The 12-Step Employment Program
for Small Businesses

The 12-Step Eployment Program
For Small Businesses

by

Patricia G. Pollack

Copyright © 1999 by Patricia G. Pollack

All rights reserved. No part of this book may be reproduced,
stored in a retrieval system, or transmitted by any means,
electronic, mechanical, photocopying, recording, or otherwise,
without written permission from the author.

ISBN 1-58500-550-9

About the Book

The 12-Step Employment Program for Small Businesses takes the mystery out of how to hire and keep good employees, as well as how to get rid of the not-so-good ones. It lights the path to a productive workforce with its logical and comprehensive step-by-step system for success. While recognizing the uniqueness of each small business, ***The 12-Step Employment Program for Small Businesses*** can be immediately implemented by every small business owner interested in taking positive action towards assembling a winning team of employees.

In plain, concise language, ***The 12-Step Employment Program for Small Businesses*** leads you through The Plan, The Job, The Pay, The Search, The Interview, The Test, The Investigation, The Offer, The Hire, The Appraisal, The Discipline, and The Termination. In addition, the book provides employment law and recordkeeping guidelines, as well as great resources for learning more about workplace issues.

This book is dedicated to Jonathan, David, and James who always make me feel like the Queen of the Universe.

Acknowledgments

This book began as a request from Sherry Cochran, who wanted to read something that would take the mystery out of how to hire and keep good employees, as well as how to get rid of the not-so-good ones. I had been teaching seminars on this subject for a number of years and shared my "handouts" with her. She was so excited by the information, she encouraged me to write it in a format that all business owners could use - a step-by-step system for success written in plain, concise language. The result was ***The 12-Step Employment Program for Small Businesses***.

So thanks Sherry, for getting me started. I also want to thank Elizabeth Miller, former business owner and Director of First Trust Bank in Charlotte, North Carolina and Maggi Braun, also a former business owner and Director of the Central Piedmont Community College Small Business Center in Charlotte, who read the initial draft of this book and gave me the benefit of their years of small business experience. Their constructive criticism made this book even more useful to the small business owner.

Most of all, thanks must be heaped upon my husband, Jonathan, who read and critiqued this book in all its various drafts. His input helped me say what I wanted to say more clearly, more simply than I thought possible.

Patricia G. Pollack

Contents

Acknowledgments ix
Introduction xiv

I. The Dilemma 1
Finding, hiring, and keeping good workers

II. The Solution 3
Introduction to the 12-Step Employment Program

III. The Program 11
12 Steps to Success

Step 1: The Plan 11
Step 2: The Job 27
Step 3: The Pay 37
Step 4: The Search 55
Step 5: The Interview 63
Step 6: The Test 73
Step 7: The Investigation 81
Step 8: The Offer 91
Step 9: The Hire 99
Step 10: The Appraisal 105
Step 11: The Discipline 111
Step 12: The Termination 125

IV. The Result 139
Conclusion

V. The Appendix 143
The Internet
The Posters
The Records

This publication, nor its contents are to be construed as legal advice.

Throughout this book, the terms "he," "she," "him" and "her" may be used interchangeably. The use of any such term shall be construed to apply to both genders.

Introduction

It is no secret that the cost of hiring a new employee can be significant. There is the cost to advertise, the cost of recruiting, the employee's salary, insurance and benefits, employer tax contribution, and the cost of training.

And what if the employee doesn't work out? In addition to starting the process all over again, you may have the cost of lost sales and missed opportunities, the cost of dissatisfied customers, and low employee morale caused by an unproductive employee. In addition, you are faced with the risk of costly lawsuits from a bad hire. It has been estimated that the cost of poor selection is as much as three times the employee's annualized compensation.

There are many publications that seek to answer the question of how to hire and retain good employees by addressing only the hiring of the employee, or by suggesting all kinds of benefits you can offer employees. In fact, these approaches look at only a small part of the employment process. There is much to think about before you hire an employee, during the employment period, and after employment ceases. Unless you are willing to view the whole employment picture, hiring and retaining good employees will remain a mystery for you.

The 12-Step Employment Program for Small Businesses takes the mystery out of how to hire and keep good employees, as well as how to get rid of the not-so-good ones. It lights the path to a productive workforce with its logical and comprehensive step-by-step system for success. While recognizing the uniqueness of each small business, ***The 12-Step Employment Program for Small Businesses*** can be immediately implemented by every small business owner interested in taking positive action towards assembling a winning team of employees.

In plain, concise language, ***The 12-Step Employment Program for Small Businesses*** leads you through The Plan, The Job, The Pay, The Search, The Interview, The Test, The Investigation, The Offer, The Hire, The Appraisal, The

Discipline, and The Termination. In addition, the book provides employment law and recordkeeping guidelines, as well as great resources for learning more about workplace issues.

The 12-Step Employment Program for Small Businesses doesn't provide you with generic answers or quick fixes. Instead, The Program requires you to think, to plan, and to discover the answer that is correct for your specific organization. Every action you take in The Program must have structure, consistency, job-relatedness, and documentation.

It may prove to be a challenge for you. But hey, you wouldn't be in business if you didn't enjoy a good challenge! So let's get started.

Chapter I

The Dilemma
Finding, hiring, and keeping good workers

I don't know what to do! I can't seem to hire good employees and I'm afraid to fire the not-so-good ones!

Finding, hiring, and keeping good workers

Hiring and firing are two words that strike fear into the hearts of even the most courageous of employers. All that goes on in between the first day of work and the day you finally finish the paperwork on a terminated employee isn't much fun either.

Much of that anxiety stems from not knowing the most effective methods of managing employees. The rest is a result of confusing and conflicting laws enacted by federal and state governments, interpreted and reinterpreted by our country's judicial system. Management ignorance and the phobia of employment litigation often results in paralysis, preventing employers from doing what they need to do to grow and prosper.

What is it, exactly, that your organization needs to grow and prosper? People. But we're not talking warm bodies here. You need productive employees that come to work on time everyday, do a good job, and want to stay with the company. And you need to get rid of everyone else without explaining yourself to a judge.

Chapter II

The Solution
Introduction to the 12-Step Employment Program

I know what I need. Just tell me how to get it!

Introduction to the 12-Step Employment Program for Small Businesses

That's what the 12-Step Employment Program for Small Businesses ("The Program") is all about - how to get and keep the people you need. Each step of The Program consists of answering a series of "catalyst" questions, designed to ignite creative solutions to common employment dilemmas. Hopefully, they will trigger additional questions for which you will seek answers. The discoveries you make will become the basis of your actions during the employment process.

The Program works within the confines of specific rules. In order for The Program to work for your company, you need to follow these rules.

Rule #1: Read this entire book.
Rule #2: Follow every step and seek the answer to every question in The Program.
Rule #3: Relate each step to the Four Principles of Effective Employee Management.
Rule #4: Be aware of all applicable Federal and State employment laws and consult a qualified employment attorney regarding compliance.

Four Principles of Effective Employee Management

Structure: Structure is the systematic framework for managing employees that you construct based on what you are trying to accomplish. In some cases, you choose the structure that's best for your organization. In other cases, the government and the courts have chosen the structure for you. Either way, the structure is what supports your decisions and actions.

Consistency: Consistency is the steadfast adherence to a course of action that results in similar situations receiving similar treatment, all in the name of a common goal. It is the principle upon which fairness and equity are based.

Job-relatedness: Job-relatedness focuses on the skills, knowledge, abilities, and behaviors that affect the employee's contribution to the organization's goal of growth and prosperity. The idea here is to concentrate your energy on what matters, and forget about everything else.

Documentation: Documentation is a written account of factual information. It is a historical record upon which future decisions and actions may be based.

FEDERAL EMPLOYMENT LAWS
This partial listing of Federal laws is not intended to be all-inclusive.

EMPLOYERS WITH ONE OR MORE EMPLOYEES:

Fair Labor Standards Act (FLSA) - governs the pay practices of all employers with employees engaged in interstate commerce.

Occupational Safety and Health Act (OSHA) - requires all employers not governed by a federally certified state plan to maintain a safe and healthy workplace and comply with specific safety standards and recordkeeping rules.

Federal Insurance Contributions Act (FICA) - requires all employers to pay Social Security and Medicare taxes, and withhold such taxes from workers' pay.

Federal Unemployment Tax Act (FUTA) - requires all employers to pay federal unemployment payroll taxes.

Equal Pay Act - requires all employers to pay men and women the same pay for the same work, while allowing for differences in merit, seniority, and incentive pay plans.

Immigration Reform and Control Act - requires all employers to hire only individuals authorized to work in the United States and prohibits discrimination based on nationality or citizenship.

Bankruptcy Act - prohibits all private employers from discriminating against an individual solely because the person has filed for bankruptcy.

Consumer Credit Protection Act - requires notification of applicants subject to credit checks, respond to applicants requesting the results of credit checks, and inform any applicant rejected based on an adverse credit report.

Employee Polygraph Protection Act - prohibits all employers engaged in interstate commerce from requiring applicants to take polygraph tests, with exceptions for positions working with certain controlled substances and certain types of security-sensitive work.

National Labor Relations Act - prohibits discrimination against employees who engage in, or who refuse to engage in union activity, and protects nonunion employees who act together to improve or protest working conditions.

Uniformed Services Employment and Reemployment Rights Act - prohibits discrimination on the basis of military obligation in hiring, job retention, and advancement and requires employers to allow individuals who enter the military for a short period of service to return to their private-sector jobs without risk of loss of seniority or benefits.

EMPLOYERS WITH 15 OR MORE EMPLOYEES:

Title VII of the Civil Rights Act of 1964 and the Civil Rights Act of 1991 - prohibits discrimination on the basis of race, color, religion, sex, or national origin.

Pregnancy Discrimination Act - prohibits employers from discriminating on the basis of pregnancy-related medical conditions.

Americans with Disabilities Act (ADA) - prohibits discrimination against disabled employees or applicants for employment.

EMPLOYERS WITH 20 OR MORE EMPLOYEES:

Age Discrimination in Employment Act (ADEA) - prohibits age discrimination against employees or applicants age 40 and older.

Consolidated Omnibus Budget Reconciliation Act (COBRA) - requires employers to make health coverage available to employees, their spouses, and their dependents upon termination of employment, death, divorce or other qualifying event at the same rate the employer would pay.

EMPLOYERS WITH 50 OR MORE EMPLOYEES:

Family and Medical Leave Act (FMLA) - requires employers to grant unpaid leave of up to 12 weeks per year for new births or adoptions, or certain medical conditions of the worker or a family member.

EMPLOYERS WITH 100 OR MORE EMPLOYEES:

Worker Adjustment and Retraining Act (WARN) - requires employers to give employees and their communities 60 days' notice of any closure or layoff affecting 50 or more full-time employees.

Chapter III

The Program
12 Steps to Success

Step 1: The Plan

12 Steps to Success - Step 1: The Plan

Imagine that you are building your dream house. You survey the land and determine your boundaries. You decide what the house will look like. You determine what resources you will need, the availability of those resources, and their cost. Based on this information, you put together a plan to build the house, then you implement that plan.

Building your dream workforce requires the same steps. You must survey the environment (the land) and determine the sphere of influence (your boundaries) by studying the external forces that affect your business, as well as auditing the internal activities of your company. You must decide what organizational structure and culture your company will assume (what the house will look like.) You must determine what skills, knowledge, and abilities (resources) you will need to build the organization (house), the supply of those skills in the labor force (the availability), and the prevailing compensation for those skills (the cost.) Based on this information, you put together a human resources plan to build the business, then implement that plan.

Human resources planning is the process of anticipating the skills, knowledge, and abilities needed for the organization to reach its goals, as well as the effective allocation of these vital resources. If done correctly, the planning process enables your company to act and change in pursuit of sustainable competitive advantage, thereby increasing your organizational capability. Taking the time to develop an effective human resources plan will increase the likelihood of a happy, productive workforce, minimize the threat of legal action, and increase the probability of long-term success.

Planning involves making assumptions about the future based on available information. This information includes external factors affecting your business, such as:
- the economy
- technology
- political and legislative issues

- social issues such as crime and education
- demographics
- prevailing wages

Searching for data on external forces is known as environmental scanning. It may start with the chambers of commerce in the markets you serve. Trade journals and business publications offer technology updates and other useful information about the business environment in which you are operating. Government census data, law enforcement crime statistics, and research conducted by employers' associations and private consultants are also excellent resources.

The offices of local government representatives can provide information about state political and legislative issues affecting your business. Free copies of United States House of Representatives bills are available to the public by writing to The House Document Room, B-18 House Annex No. 2, Washington, DC 20510 or calling (202) 225-3456. For Senate bills, written requests may be sent to The Senate Document Room, B-04 Hart Senate Office Building, Washington, DC 20510 or call (202) 224-7860.

In addition to these external forces, there are internal forces affecting your business, including:
- financial status of the company
- technological capabilities of the company
- company policies and practices
- demographics of the workforce
- absenteeism and turnover

Planning requires you to reveal the soul of your company by investigating how each of these internal forces affects your business. This process of "self-discovery" is known as internal cultural auditing.

Begin your environmental scan and internal cultural audit by asking yourself the following questions.

TO DETERMINE EXTERNAL FORCES AFFECTING YOUR BUSINESS, ASK YOURSELF

- What are the external economic forces affecting my business?
- What are the external technological forces affecting my business?
- What political and legislative issues affect my business?
- What external demographic trends affect my business?
- What social issues affect my business?
- Are the forces affecting my business limited to a city, state, region, nation, or the world?

TO DETERMINE INTERNAL FORCES AFFECTING YOUR BUSINESS, ASK YOURSELF

- What is the current financial status of my company?
- What is the current technological status of my company?
- What are my current company policies and practices?
- What are the demographics of my current workforce?
- What is the absenteeism rate of my employees?
- What is the turnover rate of my employees?

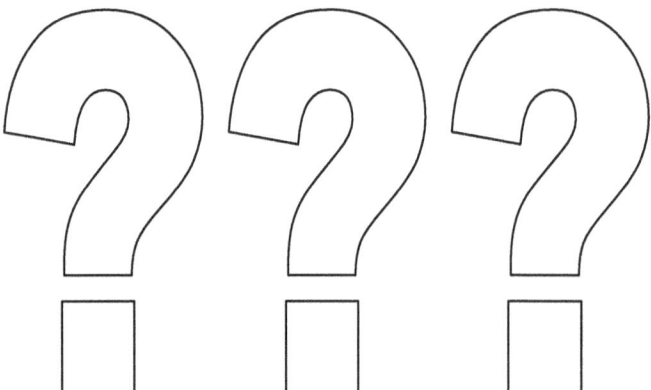

Once you have answered these questions, you are ready to decide what you want your company to look like by determining your organizational structure and culture. You may already have the structure and culture you desire, or you may decide that change is needed. To determine the most effective organizational structure and culture for your company, the following questions must be answered.

TO DETERMINE ORGANIZATIONAL STRUCTURE AND CULTURE, ASK YOURSELF

- What organizational structure will provide the strongest support for my growing business?
- What type of internal culture will provide the strongest support for my growing business?

To illustrate, let's look at how a small business may gather this information and use it to build the foundation of the company's human resources plan.

GOLDEN TOUCH ENTERPRISES

Golden Touch Enterprises is a warehousing and distribution business owned by Bob Golden. The company currently operates one warehouse which serves customers in three states. Bob expects to double the number of customers served out of the existing warehouse in the next 12 months.

To reach this goal, Bob needs information and a plan. He obtains the following data from the local Department of Labor, Employment Security Commission, Chamber of Commerce and employers' association.

· *The unemployment rate in the company's recruiting area is 4.3 percent.*

· *Prevailing wage rates for warehouse jobs in the recruiting area average $7.45 per hour.*

· *Approximately 24 percent of the local labor force has less than a high school education; 27 percent of the local labor force are high school graduates; and 19 percent of the local labor force are college graduates.*

· *There are 48 major distribution centers within a 50-mile radius of Golden Touch Enterprises.*

· *In the past five years, union elections were held in 18 of these distribution centers. Four elections resulted in union organization of warehouse employees.*

· *The local labor force is approximately 50 percent Caucasian, 35 percent Black, 10 percent Hispanic, five percent Asian, 51 percent female and 49 percent male. Approximately two percent of workers are under the age of 18 years; eight percent of workers are between 18 and 27 years old; 20 percent are between 28 and 37 years old; 40 percent are between 38 and 47 years old; 20 percent are between 48 and 57 years old; and 10 percent are 58 years or older.*

Bob contacts the local police department and discovers that last year, seven violent crimes and 50 non-violent crimes occurred for every 1000 residents. One violent crime occurred at the workplace of a local employer.

To learn more about legislative issues that may affect his plans, Bob contacts the local offices of his state representative and senator, as well as the United States Senate and House of Representatives Document Rooms. He makes a note of the following legislation under consideration:

· *Bills in both the U. S. House of Representatives and Senate that would raise the minimum wage by 50 cents in each of the next three years.*
· *A bill in the state legislature that will require employers to certify that all employees operating motor vehicles in the course of their jobs have been trained according to state guidelines and have successfully passed the state safe operator test.*

Bob thumbs through the latest issue of a magazine devoted to warehousing, distribution, and material handling and reads a story about a new method of tracking shipments. This leads Bob to search the Internet for related information. He finds several informative articles about technological advancements that can improve productivity.

Now that Bob is aware of the external forces affecting his business, he begins to audit the internal workings of the company. He reviews the company's financial statements and operational policies. He familiarizes himself with the composition of his current workforce. He studies the company's productivity to determine whether employees have the tools and technology they need to do their jobs efficiently. In addition, Bob looks at employee absenteeism and turnover to uncover any counter-productive trends that may be developing. His audit shows:

· *The company uses 36 percent of its gross revenues to pay for employee-related expenses. Employees account for approximately 85 percent of the company's total expenses.*
· *Company policies are documented and job descriptions are accurate.*

Employees are primarily white males between the ages of 21 and 40 years old with high school degrees.

Technology, tools, and equipment are adequate for the current number of customers, but may not be sufficient to handle anticipated growth.

Not counting vacations and holidays, employees average five absences per year. The turnover rate is approximately 2 percent annually.

Bob realizes that with 48 other distribution centers within commuting distance, there is a lot of competition for warehouse workers. Unemployment is low at 4.3 percent, so there are not a lot of people looking for work. There is a high probability that wages will increase as a result of a rising minimum wage and a decreasing supply of available workers. Employee-related expenses represent a large portion of the company's budget and will likely increase with higher wages and the higher training costs proposed in the state legislature. Therefore, it is imperative that Golden Touch Enterprises minimizes the number of employees needed to handle the company's growth.

Bob's internal cultural audit reveals that employees know what is expected of them, they tend to come to work on a regular basis, and they tend to stay with the company. He interprets this as the basis of a healthy internal culture, and wants to nurture this atmosphere to avoid the union activity and workplace violence other local employers are experiencing. However, Bob wants a more diverse workforce. He knows he will have to build a strong foundation of teamwork as the composition of his workforce changes.

Bob decides that his human resources plan will be based on a cross-functional team-based organizational structure that will allow team members to assume responsibility for operational policies, designing their jobs, budgeting expenses, and meeting customer requirements. He feels that in combination with an investment in the appropriate technology, this will be the most efficient structure, thus minimizing the number of employees needed to meet the company's growth targets. Furthermore, Bob feels cross-functional teams will establish a desirable and productive company culture based on employee involvement, responsibility, accountability, and respect.

Thus, the foundation of a company's human resources plan takes shape. The surrounding framework consists of determining the demand for qualified employees, the supply of those people in the labor force, and investigating the costs and benefits of alternative resources.

Determining your demand for qualified employees requires you to think about the projected market demand for your product or service, and the resources you will need to meet this demand. Implicit in this process is determining the role of technology in the productivity of your workforce.

TO DETERMINE YOUR DEMAND FOR QUALIFIED EMPLOYEES, ASK YOURSELF

- What is the projected market demand for my product or service?
- What technology must I acquire to meet future demand?
- What skills, knowledge, and abilities must I acquire to meet future demand?

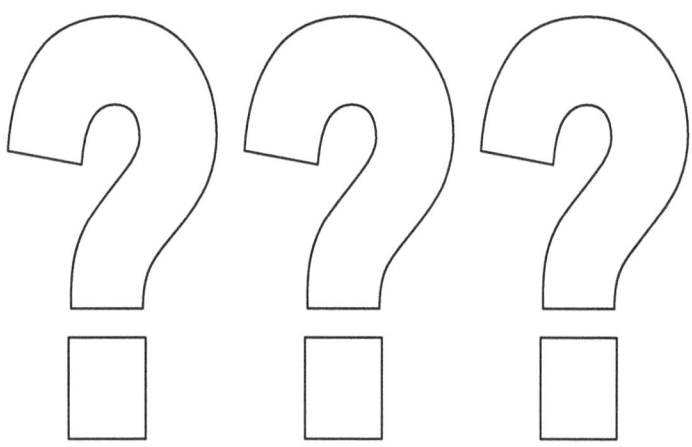

Determining the supply of qualified applicants requires you to look at your current workforce to see if you already have the employees you need, and to look at the availability of qualified applicants in the general labor force. Availability of qualified applicants in the general labor force can be gleaned from census data, information provided by chambers of commerce and employers' associations, and research by private consultants. To determine the supply of qualified applicants, try to answer these questions.

TO DETERMINE THE SUPPLY OF QUALIFIED APPLICANTS, ASK YOURSELF

- How many people within my company already possess the attributes needed?
- How many people outside the company, but within the recruiting area possess these qualifications?
- Your environmental scan should have resulted in some prevailing wage rate data. Since the cost of labor will consume a large portion of your budget, it is important to gather as much information as possible, including the costs and benefits of alternative resources. This data is available from many sources including chambers of commerce, employers' associations, trade and industry associations, staffing agencies, outplacement firms, and compensation consultants. Explore your options by searching for the answers to the following questions.

TO DETERMINE THE COST OF ALTERNATIVE RESOURCES, ASK YOURSELF

- What are the costs and benefits of hiring full-time vs. part-time employees?
- What are the costs and benefits of alternative working relationships such as employee leasing, temporary staffing, and independent contractors?
- What is the cost of available technology that could substitute for human resources?

You must find the right balance between what you need, what is available, and how much it is going to cost you. For example, if your internal supply of employees is greater than your demand for employees, your human resources plan should include a workforce reduction or "lay-off." If your demand for employees is greater than your internal supply of employees, your plan should include hiring additional workers. If the cost of labor is greater than the cost of the technology to perform the same task, your plan should substitute technology for human resources.

Finding this balance is the culmination of your human resources plan. The process can be completed by answering the following question.

TO COMPLETE YOUR HUMAN RESOURCES PLAN, ASK YOURSELF

How can I most effectively allocate the available resources to maximize productivity and meet future demand?

An effective human resources plan is fluid in nature, free to flow according to your needs. However, you must ensure it is always channeled towards the organization's goals. That means containing it, and the best way to capture your plan is through documentation. Documenting your human resources plan makes it eaaier to communicate, implement, evaluate, and change.

Here's how The Plan relates to the Four Basic Principles of Effective Employee Management:

Structure: The base of the structure consists of environmental scanning and cultural auditing. Balancing the demand, supply, and cost of qualified employees completes the framework.

Consistency: The examination of external and internal environments is performed for the sole purpose of identifying and analyzing factors affecting your company's ability to reach its goals. Likewise, balancing the demand, supply, and cost of qualified employees ensures the company has the proper resources to reach its goals.

Job-relatedness: External factors, such as the economy, technology, legislation, social concerns, demographics, and wage rates all have a significant relationship to an employee's contribution to the organization. Similarly, internal factors like absenteeism and turnover are directly related to the job.

Documentation: The plan is captured in a written record of the process and results.

Step 2: The Job

12 Steps to Success - Step 2: The Job

After developing your human resources plan, you must determine the duties, tasks, and activities that must be performed to reach the organization's goals. In addition, you must determine the knowledge, skills, and abilities required to perform this work well. The process of collecting and analyzing such objective information about the actual requirements of a job is known as job analysis.

Once the analysis is complete, you can design the jobs to enhance organizational efficiency, to reinforce your desired internal culture, and to accommodate external influences on your workforce. But first you must seek the answers to the following questions.

TO ANALYZE THE JOB, ASK YOURSELF

- What is the primary purpose of the job?
- What are the essential work activities or functions of the job?
- What specific knowledge is required to perform the essential functions of the job?
- What specific skills are required to perform the essential functions of the job?
- What specific abilities or attributes are required to perform the essential functions of the job?

TO DESIGN THE JOB, ASK YOURSELF

- Which elements of the job can be modified, combined, rearranged, or eliminated to reduce the time needed to do the job?
- How can I match equipment and work processes so they can be easily and efficiently used by employees?
- How can I create communication systems that will allow employees to experience the meaningfulness of the work performed, the responsibility for work outcomes, and knowledge of the results of the work?
- Which work processes are most effectively performed by individuals, and which are most effectively performed by teams?
- When is it more effective to use flex time, job sharing, compressed work weeks and other alternatives to traditional scheduling?

The job description is documentation of the analysis and design results. This written record of the human capital needed for success is one of the most important steps in the process of managing a business. The emphasis of a well-written description is on the ability of employees to join their collective talents in propelling the company forward, thus representing a vital link in achieving the organization's goals.

For employers subject to the Americans with Disabilities Act, the job description is also required for compliance.

The following guidelines are useful in structuring a meaningful job description.

Purpose - Clearly state the role that the person with the described set of skills or competencies plays in the process of reaching company goals. For example, *Golden Touch Enterprises strives to provide customers with products that meet their requirements for quality and price in a manner that allows the company to be increasingly profitable over time. Effective voice and data communications are essential to achieving this goal. The following competencies are required for the position of Voice/Data Communications Analyst to ensure effective voice and data communications.*

Skill Set/Competencies - Think in terms of the physical, intellectual, and social talents needed to reach company goals. Experience and education should not be confused with, or substituted for competency. For this example, competencies might include *proficiency in voice/data communications technology, excellent analytical and problem-solving skills, and excellent project planning and time management skills.*

Essential Functions - If it is not an essential function, it's a time waster and should either be automated or eliminated. All functions should have a direct relationship to company goals. For example, an essential function of this position might be *Continually evaluate technology to ensure the effective voice/data communications necessary to meet customer requirements and the financial goals of the company.*

Here's how The Job relates to the Four Basic Principles of Effective Employee Management:

Structure: The structure consists of determining the duties, tasks, and activities as well as the knowledge, skills, and abilities necessary to perform those activities. Designing jobs so that human capital is effectively allocated completes the framework.

Consistency: The analysis of job activities and competencies is conducted for the sole purpose of determining what is needed to reach the company's goals. Designing jobs for maximum effectiveness defines how the company will reach its goals.

Job-relatedness: All aspects of the analysis, design, and documentation focus on the job.

Documentation: The results of the analysis and design are documented in the job description.

SAMPLE JOB DESCRIPTION

Job Title: Accounts Payable Clerk
Reports to: Accounting Manager

PURPOSE:

Golden Touch Enterprises is committed to maintaining an excellent relationship with our suppliers. Prompt and accurate payment of accounts is essential to this goal. The following knowledge, skills, and abilities are required for the position of Accounts Payable Clerk to ensure our goals are met.

KNOWLEDGE, SKILLS, AND ABILITIES:

- Proficient in addition, subtraction, fractions, and decimals
- Proficient in manual and computer-aided bookkeeping
- Proficient in alpha/numeric data entry
- Excellent organizational skills
- Ability to plan and perform a sequence of semi-routine operations where standards of recognized procedures is available
- Ability to work effectively as a member of a cross-functional team

SAMPLE JOB DESCRIPTION

(continued)

ESSENTIAL FUNCTIONS OF THE JOB:

- Punctuality and maintenance of regular and predictable attendance according to company policy
- Ensure accuracy of all materials and supplies requisitions, receipts, and invoices
- Accurately enter invoice data into computer for prompt payment to vendors
- Print all Accounts Payable invoices, record Accounts Payable for monthly accrual, and submit this information to the Accounting Manager on a monthly basis
- Close the accounting month for Accounts Payable
- Maintain all Accounts Payable files
- Resolve vendor invoice inquiries politely, promptly, and accurately
- Abide by all company safety rules
- Miscellaneous duties as required to ensure team success

Step 3: The Pay

12 Steps to Success - Step 3: The Pay

What you compensate your employees, and how you compensate them can be the difference between the success and failure of your company. Success is achieved when you link compensation to your organization's goals.

However, linking compensation to your organization's goals requires you to know a little bit about what constitutes compensation and how the law influences it. It also requires you to explore what you hope to accomplish with your compensation plan, and how you will accomplish it.

Compensation is generally considered either direct, as in wages and salaries, or indirect, as in company-sponsored health insurance and government-mandated programs like Social Security. Direct compensation is usually referred to as "pay" and indirect compensation is usually referred to as "benefits."

Direct compensation can be further described as "fixed" or "base" pay and "variable" or "incentive" pay. For example, a monthly salary would be considered base pay and a sales commission would be considered incentive pay.

The Fair Labor Standards Act (FLSA), and its interpretation by the Department of Labor (DOL) is the primary regulatory statute when it comes to pay. Among other things, the FLSA specifies the minimum wage and exceptions to the minimum, maximum hours and overtime rules, recordkeeping regulations, and child labor provisions. In addition to the FLSA, you must adhere to Wage and Hour laws for the states in which you operate.

It is not within the scope of this publication to explain all the provisions and resulting interpretations of compensation law. However, there are some common misconceptions that are worthy of discussion.

For example, a mistake often made by employers is to assume that if you pay employees a salary, you don't have to pay them overtime. The FLSA specifies categories of employees that are considered exempt from overtime. Each category is defined according to the responsibilities and duties of the position. Some of the exemptions specified in the FLSA are outlined below.

Executive exemption - ALL of the following must be met:
1. Primary duty is management of the enterprise, department, or subdivision
2. Customarily and regularly directs the work of at least two other employees
3. Authority to hire or fire, or whose recommendation to hire and fire is given particular weight
4. Customarily and regularly exercise discretionary powers
5. Devotes no more than 40 percent of hours to activities not directly and closely related to managerial duties
6. Paid at least $155 per week exclusive of board, lodging or other facilities

Administrative exemption - ALL of the following tests must be met:
1. Office or nonmanual work directly related to the management or business operations of the employer or the employer's customers OR work that is directly related to academic instruction or training in a school or educational establishment
2. Customarily and regularly exercises discretion and independent judgment, as distinguished from using skills and following procedures, and must have the authority to make important decisions
3. Regularly assists a proprietor or a bona fide executive or administrative employee OR performs work under only general supervision along specialized or technical lines requiring special training, experience or knowledge OR executes under only general supervision special assignments
4. Devotes less than 40 percent of hours to work not directly and closely related to administrative duties
5. Paid at least $155 per week

Professional exemption - ALL of the following tests must be met:
1. Work requires knowledge of an advanced type in a field of science or learning, customarily obtained by a prolonged course of specialized instruction and study OR work that is original and creative in character in a recognized field of artistic endeavor and the result of which depends primarily on the employee's invention, imagination, or talent OR work as a certified teacher in a school or educational institution.
2. Consistently exercises discretion and judgment
3. Work is predominantly intellectual and varied, as distinguished from routine or mechanical duties
4. Devotes less than 20 percent of the time worked on activities not essentially a part of and necessarily incident to professional duties
5. Paid at least $170 per week

Although the determination of whether a job qualifies as "exempt" under the FLSA is not clear cut, here is an example of how one company went through the decision-making process.

Golden Touch Enterprises has a position called "Warehouse Supervisor." The job entails coordinating the work schedules of material handlers, and supervising the work activities of the warehouse employees. The Warehouse Supervisor is very experienced in warehousing and distribution, and is allowed considerable leeway in running the operation. However, because the company is small, the Warehouse Supervisor spends over half of the time loading and unloading pallets, packing boxes, and loading trucks. In addition to these manual duties, the Warehouse Supervisor is responsible for reviewing and maintaining proper shipping and receiving records. The pay for this position is $480 per week.

Bob Golden performed the following analysis to determine whether this position should be exempt from the overtime provisions of the FLSA:

Warehouse Supervisor: Executive exemption
ALL *of the following tests must be met:*

1. *Primary duty is management of the enterprise, department, or subdivision - **FAIL** - Although this position is responsible for the work activities of employees, its primary activity is not management.*
2. *Customarily and regularly directs the work of at least two other employees - PASS - Supervises at least two other employees.*
3. *Authority to hire or fire, or whose recommendation to hire and fire is given particular weight - PASS - Does have this authority*
4. *Customarily and regularly exercise discretionary powers - PASS - This position has considerable autonomy and therefore is required to exercise discretionary power on a daily basis.*
5. *Devotes no more than 40 percent of his hours to activities not directly and closely related to managerial duties - PASS - More than 40 percent of the hours worked are devoted to non-managerial duties.*
6. *Paid at least $155 per week exclusive of board, lodging or other facilities - PASS - Salary exceeds this minimum.*

According to Bob's analysis, this position does NOT meet the requirements for Executive exemption because although this position is responsible for the work activities of employees, its primary activity is not management, thus failing the very first test. He performed the following analysis to see if an administrative exemption was appropriate.

Warehouse Supervisor: Administrative exemption
ALL of the following tests must be met:

1. *Office or nonmanual work directly related to the management or business operations of the employer or the employer's customers OR work that is directly related to academic instruction or training in a school or educational establishment - PASS - This position has responsibility for shipping, receiving, and related recordkeeping.*
2. *Customarily and regularly exercises discretion and independent judgment, as distinguished from using skills and following procedures, and must have the authority to make important decisions - PASS - This position has considerable autonomy and therefore is required to exercise discretion and independent judgment on a daily basis.*
3. *Regularly assists a proprietor or a bona fide executive or administrative employee OR performs work under only general supervision along specialized or technical lines requiring special training, experience or knowledge OR executes under only general supervision special assignments -PASS - This position performs work under only general supervision along specialized, technical lines requiring special training, experience, and knowledge.*
4. *Devotes less than 40 percent of his hours to work not directly and closely related to administrative duties -* **FAIL** *- Devotes over 40 percent of the time worked to non-administrative duties*
5. *Paid at least $155 per week - PASS - Salary exceeds the minimum.*

Once again, Bob's analysis indicates that this position does NOT meet the test for Administrative exemption because over 40 percent of the time worked is devoted to non-administrative duties. He proceeded to look at the possiblity of a professional exemption, as illustrated in the following analysis.

Warehouse Supervisor: Professional exemption
ALL of the following tests must be met:

1. *Work requires knowledge of an advanced type in a field of science or learning, customarily obtained by a prolonged course of specialized instruction and study OR work that is original and creative in character in a recognized field of artistic endeavor and the result of which depends primarily on the employee's invention, imagination, or talent OR work as a certified teacher in a school or educational institution -* **FAIL** *- No such education is required.*
2. *Consistently exercises discretion and judgment -PASS - This position has considerable autonomy and therefore is required to exercise discretion and independent judgment on a daily basis.*
3. *Work is predominantly intellectual and varied, as distinguished from routine or mechanical duties -* **FAIL** *- Although the work is varied, this test distinguishes intellectual work from the manual work of this position.*
4. *Devotes less than 20 percent of the time worked on activities not essentially a part of and necessarily incident to his professional duties -* **FAIL** *- Devotes more than 20 percent of his time on manual duties.*
5. *Paid at least $170 per week - PASS - Salary exceeds the minimum*

As a result of this analysis, Bob decided that the position did not meet the requirements of professional exemption either. Therefore, it was subject to the overtime provisions of the FLSA, and that the Warehouse Supervisor would be paid 1 1/2 times the hourly rate for all hours over 40 worked in a week.

In addition to the Executive, Administrative, and Professional exemptions, Computer Professionals may be exempt from overtime. The Small Business Job Protection Act (SBJPA) states that computer professionals who are paid at least

$27.63 per hour and whose primary duties include certain types of activities are exempted from the overtime provisions of the FLSA. According to section 2105 (a) of the SBJPA, an exempted computer professional is "a computer systems analyst, computer programmer, software engineer, or other similarly skilled worker whose primary duty is:

(A) the application of systems analysis techniques and procedures, including consulting with users, to determine hardware, software, or system functional specifications;

(B) the design, development, documentation, analysis, creation, testing, or modification of computer systems or programs, including prototypes, based on and related to user or system design specifications;

(C) the design, documentation, testing, creation, or modification of computer programs related to machine operating systems; or

(D) a combination of duties described in subparagraphs (A), (B), and (C) the performance of which requires the same level of skills; and who, in the case of an employee who is compensated on an hourly basis, is compensated at a rate of not less than $27.63 an hour.

Furthermore, the FLSA allows certain commissioned retail employees an exemption from overtime. Under section 7(I) of the FLSA, commissioned retail employees are exempt from overtime if:

(A) the employees work at a retail establishment AND

(B) the employees' regular rate is more than 1.5 time the minimum wage AND

(C) over a representative period of at least a month, the employees earn more than 50 percent of their compensation from commissions on goods or services.

If the employee is exempt from the overtime provisions of the FLSA, then:
1. compensation is for the job, not the hours.
2. compensatory time for hours worked over 40 in a week may be granted at the discretion of the company.

3. employees must generally receive full salary for any week in which services are performed without regard to the number of days or hours worked in order to be considered "exempt." An exception to this requirement permits deductions for absences of a day or more due to illness if the deduction is made in accordance with a bona fide plan, policy or practice. Thus, the employer must have a plan, policy or practice concerning absences and it is preferable that the plan be in writing in a company policy manual or employee handbook. If there is such a plan, then once employees have exhausted their paid days off, the employer may allow future days off without pay if the absence is a day or more.

If the employee is subject to the overtime provisions of the FLSA, or "non-exempt", then:
1. 1 1/2 times the employee's base rate must be paid for all hours worked over 40 in a work week. The FLSA does not regulate how many hours in a day, just in the work week.
2. paid holidays, and paid vacation days are not counted as hours worked but are paid whether worked or not. Overtime kicks in only when the employee actually works over 40 hours.
3. you may not grant compensatory time in lieu of overtime. You may not prohibit payment for unauthorized hours worked or unauthorized overtime. Employees cannot be engaged in any work which would benefit the employer without being duly compensated, regardless of whether that work was authorized.

The law also affects indirect compensation, or benefits. For example, there are legally mandated benefits, such as Old-Age, Survivors, Disability, and Health Insurance, Railroad Retirement Benefits, Unemployment Compensation, and Workers' Compensation. Group health insurance plans are regulated by the Employee Retirement Income Security Act (ERISA), the Health Maintenance Organization Act, the Consolidated Omnibus

Budget Reconciliation Act (COBRA), the Health Insurance Portability and Accountability Act, the 1993 Omnibus Budget Reconciliation Act, and federal antidiscrimination laws.

Obviously, you must comply with the various compensation-related regulations, but they should not be your primary concern. Your focus must be on the relationship between compensation and your company's goals. To make that connection, you must answer the following questions.

TO LINK COMPENSATION TO GOALS, ASK YOURSELF

- How will I evaluate jobs to determine their relative worth to my organization? What role will this evaluation play in my overall compensation plan?
- What role will compensation play in attracting and retaining employees?
- What role will compensation play in rewarding past performance and encouraging future performance?
- How much money will the company commit to compensation? How is this money best allocated?
- Are company stock options a viable alternative to traditional compensation?
- Will the company offer indirect compensation, or benefits to employees? If so, which benefits will be offered and how will they be structured?
- Will any of these benefits be offered to unmarried domestic partners or adult family members living with the employee?
- Will compensation be administered internally or through an external administrator?

To ensure your compensation retains its strong link to your organization's goals, you must capture it in writing. Documentation of your compensation structure allows you to continually monitor it to evaluate its effectiveness and change it as needed. Written records of compensation, such as time cards and sheets ensure that compensation practices are consistent with the overall structure.

Documentation of your compensation practices is also an important aspect of compliance with Federal and State employment laws. For example, the FLSA requires employers to "make, keep, and preserve . . records of the persons employed by him and of the wages, hours, and other conditions and practices of employment maintained by him . . ."

Here's how The Pay relates to the Four Basic Principles of Effective Employee Management:

Structure: The structure consists of how much employees will be directly and indirectly compensated relative to the industry, the community, and fellow employees.

Consistency: Consistency is achieved via the direct linkage between compensation and organization goals.

Job-relatedness: Job-relatedness focuses on the relative worth of the job to the organization, and the role compensation plays in attracting and retaining employees, rewarding past performance, and encouraging future performance.

Documentation: Documentation includes the written record of the compensation structure, as well as time cards and sheets.

REAL QUESTIONS - REAL ANSWERS

The following questions came from small business owners grappling with the intracacies of employee pay.

1. Do we have to use a time clock for our employees?

The use of time clocks is not required. However, the Fair Labor Standards Act (FLSA) does require that employers keep accurate records of the hours worked by employees covered by its overtime provisions. Exempt employees are not subject to this requirement because they are paid for the job, not the number of hours worked.

The method in which you keep these records is a matter of preference. Many employers feel that time clocks, especially computerized time clocks are the easiest and most accurate method of record keeping. Other employers prefer a less structured culture where employees manually record their time worked on time sheets.

The crucial point to remember is that the time recorded must accurately reflect time worked.

2. Can I "round" the minutes my employees work to the nearest quarter hour?

Rounding is a common and legally accepted practice as long as the employer is consistent about rounding equally at both the beginning and the end of the shift. However, rounding must not result in the employee working more than one hour per week for which he is not paid. This is a possibility with the employee who consistently clocks in a few minutes early and clocks out a few minutes late, but never enough to round up to the next quarter hour of compensation. Working more than one hour per week without compensation is considered a form of working off the clock and violates the law.

The most effective solution to this problem is to shrink the increments used for rounding. Rounding to the nearest tenth of an hour makes it more difficult to unintentionally violate this provision of the law than rounding to the nearest quarter hour.

> 3. *I am trying to control payroll costs by limiting overtime. Can I refuse payment for unauthorized overtime?*

In an effort to reign in labor costs, many employers develop policies prohibiting payment for unauthorized hours worked or unauthorized overtime. It is illegal for a company to have such a policy. Furthermore, the employee cannot be engaged in any work which would benefit the employer without being duly compensated, regardless of whether that work was authorized.

For example, let's say you're working on a major proposal for a client. The deadline is approaching quickly, and you need the final draft typed. Your Administrative Assistant, a salaried non-exempt employee, takes it upon himself to take the proposal home and type it on his computer. At the end of the week, he turns in his time sheet with the hours he worked at home included. You exclaim, "No one asked you to do this! And I didn't authorize it!" Does the company have to pay that employee? You bet!

So how do you keep payroll costs under control if employees can rack up unauthorized hours that the company is forced to pay? Develop, document, and clearly communicate a policy that prohibits salaried non-exempt and hourly employees from working unauthorized hours. The policy should specify the disciplinary consequences of working unauthorized hours. Discipline may include warnings and termination of employment, but it may not prohibit payment for working unauthorized hours.

> **4.** *When I hire employees, I issue them uniforms, keys, locks for their lockers, and other company property. Often when they leave the company, they don't return the property. Can I either deny delivery of their final paycheck, or require automatic payroll deduction for company-issued property not returned upon termination of employment?*

Remember, you must pay for hours worked according to the FLSA, so you can not deny payment by holding a paycheck indefinitely. Furthermore, many state laws require a signed employee authorization before such deductions can be made from a paycheck. The best thing to do is have the employee sign an authorization to deduct the value of any company property not returned. This should be done on the employee's first day of work, or when the company property is issued to them.

5. *Suppose an exempt employee notifies management that she plans to work only one half day. Is it legal to apply that half-day against her paid days off?*

The law is unclear on this subject. The regulations generally discuss absences of a day or more. If an employee is absent from work for a full day for personal reasons, his or her salary status will not be affected if deductions are made for the day, regardless of whether the day is charged against paid days off. The regulations do not address half-day absences. Some courts have found that allowing exempt employees half-days off and applying them to their paid days off to be a violation of the salary basis and thereby jeopardizes their exempt status. On the other hand, some courts have found no violation. Because of these conflicting rulings, some attorneys advise that a prudent course of conduct is not to have a half-day policy, paid or unpaid, in connection with exempt employees.

6. *What is the law regarding "docking" the pay of exempt employees when they have exhausted all their paid days off? Is it necessary (and legal) to outline, in a company policy manual, that in the event employees do exhaust all paid days off, they are eligible for X number of unpaid days off?*

Employees must generally receive full salary for any week in which services are performed without regard to the number of days or hours worked in order to be considered "exempt." An exception to this requirement permits deductions for absences of a day or more due to illness if the deduction is made in accordance with a bona fide plan, policy or practice. Thus, the employer must have a plan, policy or practice concerning absences and it is preferable that the plan be in writing in a company policy manual or employee handbook. If there is such a plan, then once employees have exhausted their paid days off, the employer may allow future days off without pay if the absence is a day or more.

So, you can have a specific written policy that says that exempt employees are eligible for X paid sick days a year, and that once those days have been exhausted, additional sick days will be unpaid. A common way to handle this is to have a Leave of Absence Policy (consistent with the Family Medical Leave Act where applicable) that requires prior approval in order to be considered an excused absence. Unexcused absences, of course, would be subject to disciplinary action. That way you don't have to set an arbitrary limit to the number of unpaid days, yet you retain control of the situation.

7. *Can you grant college credit in lieu of pay for student interns?*

If the internship experience is structured strictly to enhance the intern's training and experience, and no employees were displaced by the intern, alternative methods of compensation may in some cases be permissible. However, courts have ruled that interns cannot waive their rights under FSLA by signing an employment contract that grants a stipend or educational credits in lieu of wages.

Step 4: The Search

12 Steps to Success - Step 4: The Search

Recruiting the ideal employee requires an organized, targeted search plan that includes determining what qualifications you need for the job, as well as where to search for qualified applicants. A good place to start is with the job description (Step 2: The Job.) It is an excellent resource to assist you with answering the following questions.

TO DETERMINE FOR WHOM YOU ARE SEARCHING, ASK YOURSELF

- What are the general requirements for the job? What are the basic knowledge, skills and abilities required?
- What are the attributes of employees who succeeded in the job in the past, as well as those who did not? What traits and behaviors does this job require?
- What technical competencies does this job require?

You may choose to enlist the help of a professional search firm to assist you with your recruiting efforts. Fees for such search services vary according to location, industry, position level and other factors. Currently, search fees are averaging approximately 30 percent of the new employee's first year's salary.

If you decide to conduct the search yourself, answering the following questions will help you to concentrate your efforts on reaching your target audience.

TO DETERMINE WHERE TO SEARCH, ASK YOURSELF

- What is the primary source of information for individuals with the qualifications I seek? Do they read the local newspaper? Which sections of the paper do they read? Do they listen to a particular radio station? Do they subscribe to specific magazines or newsletters? Do they use the Internet as a source of information? If so, which sites are they visiting most often?
- When do these individuals seek information? Do they read the morning paper or the evening paper? Do they listen to the radio in the morning, mid-day, evening, or late night?
- Where do these individuals gather to discuss topics of interest? Are they members of professional, civic, or social organizations? Do they attend trade shows?
- Do these individuals use public employment services or college placement services to gather information about career opportunities?
- Are current employees a viable source for referring qualified applicants?

Use this information to develop your recruitment campaign, and document how you will implement it. A written plan of action will help you to be more consistent in your recruitment efforts and enables you to more easily assess, adjust, and improve the search process in the future. Be sure to include how you will:

a) communicate the knowledge, skills, abilities, traits, behaviors, and technical competencies you require in your employment advertising.
b) communicate your requirements in the location most likely to reach your targeted applicants.
c) communicate your requirements at the time most likely to reach your targeted applicants.
d) communicate your requirements via the media most likely to reach your targeted applicants.

Once your message reaches your intended audience, interested individuals will contact the company by telephone, fax, e-mail, U. S. mail, or in person. It will be up to you to cull through all these potential candidates to find qualified applicants. The initial screening process consists of asking yourself the following questions:

TO FIND QUALIFIED APPLICANTS, ASK

- Does this individual appear to have the basic knowledge, skills, and competencies required?
- Does this individual exhibit the attributes required for success in this job?
- Does this individual appear to have the technical competencies this job requires?

Those that appear to be qualified for the job, and who you wish to interview should complete an employment application, even if they have submitted a resume. A well-designed employment application provides a consistent structure for gathering data, as well as legally defensible certifications and authorizations necessary for the employment process. An example of statements you may choose to appear on your application follows. Consult a knowledgeable employment attorney to assist you with the wording that is most appropriate for your company.

I certify that the above information is true and I understand that falsification will be grounds for rejection of this application or, if discovered after hire, termination of employment.

I give my permission for past employers, references, and educational institutions listed on this form to be contacted for the purpose of verifying my credentials, work experience, and job qualifications.

I understand that if I am hired, employment with the company is "at-will" and that employment can be terminated at any time and for any reason by either myself or the employer.

---

*Here's how The Search relates to the
Four Basic Principles of Effective Employee Management:*

Structure: The foundation of the structure consists of determining for whom, and where you are searching. The communication, screening, and application processes complete the framework.

Consistency: Consistency is achieved by standardizing effective processes and concentrating on the specific qualifications needed to reach the organization's goals.

Job-relatedness: All aspects of the search are geared towards seeking job-related qualifications.

Documentation: Documentation takes the form of a written recruitment campaign, as well as the application form which records vital information.

"Do Nothing" Technology Helps You Find Candidates Online

Wondering how to quickly find qualified job candidates online with minimal effort? Maybe you should let a "spider" do the work.

With millions of resumes floating around on the Internet, and limited time on the part of small business owners to search every site to find a good match, many employers are turning to resume spiders. These automated agents track down the newest resumes posted on the Internet and automatically e-mail a greeting from the client company to potential candidates. The result is a greater number of qualified candidates in a relatively short period of time with little effort.

Resume Robot, offered by Information Techology Talent Association is one such spider service. There are a few others, including Resume Replicator offered by CareerCast which spiders the Internet for resumes on personal homepages, free resume databases and usenet groups and replicates them on the CareerCast website. As employers become more comfortable using spiders, the number of online recruiting sites that offer spidering services will increase accordingly.

Spidering services are not free, of course. Costs run from $600 to $7200 per year, depending on how the service is configured. But for a busy employer eager to find good candidates quickly, it may well be worth the investment.

Step 5: The Interview

12 Steps to Success - Step 5: The Interview

Interview styles vary dramatically depending on the interviewer, the interviewee, and the interpersonal dynamics between them. And because of these dynamics and the personal relationship that develops during an interview, employers often refer to the resulting "gut feel" that led them to a particular employment decision.

Short of evisceration, there is no way to eliminate your "gut." However, effective interviews can be conducted regardless of the unique styles of the individuals involved and in spite of the natural tendency to form a subjective opinion about the applicant.

Research and experience have shown that structured interviews provide much more consistent and job-related information about an applicant's qualifications than unstructured interviews. A written interview guide can transform a meandering discussion into a cohesive, fact-finding mission. The result is an effective interview that allows for individual style and provides an objective balance to your "gut-feel."

To provide structure for the interview, you must answer the following questions.

TO PROVIDE STRUCTURE FOR THE INTERVIEW, ASK YOURSELF

- What initial impression of the company do you want to convey to the applicant?
- What specific questions about relevant skills or areas of knowledge will reveal the applicant's level of competency in those areas?
- How will you encourage the applicant to discuss occupational interests and career goals?
- How will you encourage the applicant to verbally explore personal and professional strengths and weaknesses, working relationships with co-workers, supervisors, and subordinates, and other attributes?
- How will you ensure that both you and the applicant have sufficient information to make an intelligent decision as to whether or not to proceed to the next step in the employment process?
- What final impression of the company do you want to leave with the applicant?

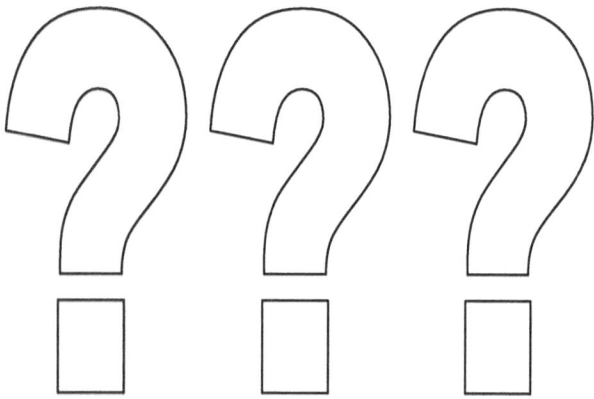

There are four major types of interview questions:

1. Credentials: Questions about experience, education, training, degrees and certificates, such "What accounting courses have you taken?" or "What experience do you have in operating heavy equipment?"
2. Opinions: Questions soliciting the candidate's opinions about work-related topics, such as "What do you think is the best approach to settling differences with co-workers?" or "Which method of organizing multiple projects works best for you?"
3. Knowledge: Questions to assess the candidate's technical knowledge required for job performance, such as "What are the steps involved in processing a payment by check?" or "What are the primary safety considerations in operating a forklift?"
4. Situational/Behavioral: Questions designed to assess how the candidate will respond to situations that may be encountered on the job, such as "Suppose you and another coworker are jointly responsible for completing an assignment. Your coworker is not doing his or her share of the work. What would you do?" or "Tell me about a supervisor you have not gotten along with, and the most difficult interaction that you had with that supervisor."

Typically, you will want to ask follow-up questions to probe deeper into the subject being explored. However, you should not allow the follow-up questions to distract you from the structured organization of the interview.

It is important to collect the same information from each candidate. This will allow you to more effectively compare candidates and make a better hiring choice.

No part of the interview may discriminate, or be interpreted as discriminating against a legally protected class or group of people. You may not ask questions relating to:

- age or birthdate
- religion
- race
- marital status
- number of children or who will care for them
- parents
- residence
- health status
- psychological well-being
- financial obligations
- previous arrests
- memberships in social organizations
- visible characteristics

However, you may ask about:
- job experience and job duties
- reasons for termination
- references
- work schedules
- career interests
- education
- job training
- qualifications for the job
- if they've been convicted of a crime

SAMPLE INTERVIEW DOs AND DON'Ts:

DO ASK -
- If you are younger than 18, do you have the necessary work permit?
- What level of education have you completed?

DON'T ASK -
- How old are you?

- When did you graduate from high school (or college)?

DO ASK -
- To which job-related professional organizations do you belong?

DON'T ASK –
- To which clubs, societies, or other organizations do you belong?

DO ASK -
- Can you perform the following essential functions of the job: frequent overnight travel? regular and predictable attendance? lifting 50-pound bags? speaking fluent Spanish? working on Saturdays?

DON'T ASK -
- Do you have any children? How old are your children? What are your child care arrangements?
- How many days of sick leave did you take last year?
- Do you have any disabilities? Have you ever received workers' compensation or disability payments?
- Where were you (your parents, your spouse) born? How did you learn to speak Spanish?
- Do you belong to a religion that would prevent you from working on Saturdays?

DO ASK -
- Do you have reliable transportation for the travel required by the job?
- What's your current address? How long have you lived there? What was your previous address?

DON'T ASK -
- Do you own a car?

- Do you own or rent your home? Have you ever lived outside this country?

Your questions, the candidate's responses, the follow-up discussion, and your evaluation of the applicant should be noted during the interview. This allows you to document the facts as you uncover them, and ensures a more reliable comparison between candidates.

Interview notes can include general attitude, presentation, professional dress and ability to express ideas. However, notes taken during the interview can not include any discriminatory information, including observations of the applicant's physical characteristics, speaking or mannerisms that are based upon race, color, religion, sex, or national origin even if it is volunteered.

Here's how The Interview relates to the Four Basic Principles of Effective Employee Management:

Structure: Structure is provided by the interview guide, which includes an introduction, technical questions, personal and interpersonal questions, and closing comments.

Consistency: Consistency is achieved via a standardized interview process that concentrates on evaluating the qualifications required to reach the organization's goals.

Job-relatedness: All aspects of the interview are geared towards relating applicants' knowledge, skills, and abilities to the essential functions of the job.

Documentation: The interview guide, applicant responses and follow-up discussions, and job-related evaluations are recorded.

Step 6: The Test

12 Steps to Success - Step 6: The Test

It is widely recognized that when you take the time to find a good match between employee and job, that employee will be more productive and stay with the company. And increasingly, employers are turning to pre-employment tests to assist them in this cause.

The primary reason for integrating tests into the selection process is to increase the level of information available for decision making. Tests should be supplemental to the application data and the personal interview.

One reason some employers are hesitant to utilize pre-employment testing is fear of litigation. They worry about the legality of testing. However, as long as the test meets federal guidelines, it is legal.

The Uniform Guidelines on Employment Selection Procedures (UGESP) state that any selection process which adversely impacts employment opportunities for any protected group should be validated. Notice that there are two distinct concepts of which you should be aware: (1) adverse impact; and (2) validity.

Adverse impact is generally defined as when the selection rate of any race, sex or ethnic group is less than 80 percent of the rate for the group with the highest selection rate. So, say you have 30 jobs to fill and 100 applicants, 60 of whom are White and 40 of whom are Black. If the group with the highest selection rate is White, and you select 30 percent or 18 of the White applicants, then it might be considered adverse impact if the selection rate of Blacks is less than 24 percent or fewer than nine Black applicants.

To take this example one step further, suppose your selection rate is less than 24 percent or fewer than nine Black applicants. The UGESP requires that you prove that your selection tool is valid. If your selection tool is proven to be valid, then you are not violating employment discrimination laws by using it, even if it has an adverse impact on a protected group.

Validity is proof that the test is measuring what it is supposed to measure. Validation can be achieved through three methods:
1. Content validity - the content of the test is representative of the content of the job itself.
2. Criterion validity - there is a statistical relationship between scores on a test and levels or measures of job performance.
3. Construct validity - the test actually measures an identified trait that is important to the successful performance of the job.

Employers should always investigate the validity of a test before using it. Ask when the test was validated, and under what conditions the validation was performed. For example, a test that was validated in 1955 using a sample of Harvard University graduate students may not be valid for testing a population of applicants today who have no college education.

One other factor you should consider is whether the test is reliable. In other words, does it consistently measure what it is supposed to measure? Or, do the results change with multiple administrations of the test? The reliability of the test is crucial to determining its worth in the selection process.

Another reason employers hesitate to utilize pre-employment testing is the plethora of assessment and profiling products on the market, and the uncertainty regarding which ones to use. To ease the confusion, it helps to understand a little bit about their varying purposes, and how they can assist you in the selection process.

First of all, pre-employment tests are developed to measure different aspects of the applicant. The most common are honesty and integrity tests, attitude tests, personality tests, skills tests, and job fit tests.

Honesty and integrity tests identify applicants that have high propensities to steal, use drugs, and not come to work on a regular basis. They can be useful as an initial screening device since they often weed out controlled substance users before you go through the expense of a chemical drug test. However, you must be diligent in your search for a test that is not culturally biased.

Attitude tests typically assess an applicant's attitudes toward attendance, safety, customer service, violence, quality, teamwork, supervision, and many other areas. Useful information can be revealed through attitude tests, including a tendency toward violence and disdain for authority figures. As with honesty and integrity tests, you must be sure that the test you are using harbors no cultural bias.

Personality tests tend to group individuals into personality styles, such as Introvert/Extrovert, Cooperative/Competitive, Challenger/Adapter and so forth. They often use sets of words or phrases, requiring the participant to select the appropriate word or phrase.

Skills testing is crucial to the selection process. There are excellent tools on the market to assess clerical, technical, and mechanical skills. Skill tests are difficult to fake, and tend to be good indicators of the applicant's technical competency.

Job fit tests typically take a more holistic approach to selection than the other types of tests. They may assess the cognitive abilities, skills, interests, and personality traits of an applicant and compare that to the cognitive abilities, skills, interests, and personality traits of someone who has successfully performed the job in the past. Job fit tests often provide in-depth information and a framework around which you can base your hiring decision.

To determine which pre-employment test, or combination of tests will give you the information you need, you must answer the following questions.

TO DETERMINE THE APPROPRIATE TEST, ASK

Will the test give me a valid and reliable measure of whether the applicant possesses:
1. the knowledge
2. the technical skills
3. the social skills
4. the physical abilities
5. the cognitive abilities
6. the personality traits
7. the occupational interests

Necessary to perform the essential functions of the job?

Proper, consistent administration of the test is crucial. Variations in administration will produce meaningless test results. Written administration guidelines are useful in maintaining consistency during the testing process. The guidelines should address the following factors, as well as any others that may affect test results:
1. the person administering the test
2. the environment in which the test is administered (i.e. space, light, noise, and temperature)
3. the manner in which instructions are delivered
4. the time allowed for completion of the test

Documentation of the test administration and results will provide a record of each candidate's performance, allowing you to easily compare candidates' qualifications with the essential functions of the job. In addition, this documentation is required by the laws prohibiting discrimination in employment.

Here's how The Test relates to the Four Basic Principles of Effective Employee Management:

Structure: The structure consists of the systematic process of determining job-related knowledge, skills, abilities, and traits that you will assess. The assessment method and the administration of that assessment complete the framework.

Consistency: Consistency is achieved through the steadfast adherence to a reliable testing process that will measure the attributes required for the organization to achieve its goals.

Job-relatedness: Only tests that are valid tools in assessing the qualifications needed to perform the essential functions of the job are used.

Documentation: The test, the administration of the test, and the test results are documented.

Step 7: The Investigation

12 Steps to Success - Step 7: The Investigation

Nearly one quarter of all resumes, and corresponding applications include false information. The most common form of deception involves overstating the applicant's education. Second in frequency is inflation of job responsibilities.

Background checks can often uncover these lies. You may be thinking, "Why bother? Past employers won't tell me anything!" However, with a well-designed investigation system, and questions that are directly related to the qualifications for the job, your chances of getting the information you need increase dramatically.

The investigation can be conducted internally by a member of your organization or externally by a professional investigative service. If you use an external service, it does not reduce your potential liability for errors made during the reference-checking process. The investigative service is your agent, and you can be held liable for the actions of your agents.

The most effective way to validate background information is to use preprinted forms with fill-in-the-blank statements for verifying education, former place of employment, and so forth. Include a section that authorizes the release of the information, and have the applicant sign it, or photocopy the signed authorization from the application. Send the forms to former companies and schools. Follow up with each reference by phone if you don't get your answers within a reasonable time.

SAMPLE VERIFICATION FORM - EDUCATION

TO: University of Tennessee
Records/Transcripts
FROM: Bob Golden, Golden Touch Enterprises
SUBJECT: Verification of Education

The following individual has applied for employment with our company and has authorized the release of the following information so that we may verify his/her education.

(Name of applicant printed here)

_____

I give my permission for past employers, references, and educational institutions to be contacted for the purpose of verifying my credentials, work experience, and job qualifications.

_____   _____
Signature of Applicant   *Date*

Please complete this form and fax it to: Bob Golden, Golden Touch Enterprises, 704-555-7065.

Dates enrolled: __/__/____   to   __/__/____

Graduation date: __/__/____

Degree Received: _____

_____   _____
Name of the individual completing this form Phone number

SAMPLE VERIFICATION FORM
WORK HISTORY

TO: Beta Software Company
FROM: Bob Golden, Golden Touch Enterprises
SUBJECT: Verification of Work History

The following individual has applied for employment with our company and has authorized the release of the following information so that we may verify his/her work history.

(name of applicant printed here)

_____

I give my permission for past employers, references, and educational institutions to be contacted for the purpose of verifying my credentials, work experience, and job qualifications.

_____   _____
Signature of Applicant   *Date*

Please complete the back of this form and fax it to:
Bob Golden, Golden Touch Enterprises, 704-555-7065.

SAMPLE VERIFICATION FORM *(continued)*
WORK HISTORY

Dates employed: ___/___/_____ - ___/___/_____

Position titles and dates held:

_____   ___/___/___ - ___/___/___
_____   ___/___/___ - ___/___/___

Reason for termination of employment:

_____

How would you describe this employee's performance?

_____

How would you describe this employee's attendance?

_____

How would you describe this employee's ability to work with co-workers?

_____

Would you rehire this employee? Why or why not?

_____

_____   _____
Name of the individual completing this form   *Phone number*

You can't ask the former employer anything that the law doesn't permit you to ask the applicant. That includes questions regarding age, birthdate, religion, race, marital status, children or child care arrangements, parents, residence, health status, psychological well-being, financial obligations, previous arrests, memberships in social organizations, or visible characteristics.

In addition to verifying that the information on the application is correct, credit checks are good to use whenever personal financial conduct is relevant. A consumer credit report retrieves reported credit data from a credit reporting agency. For more in-depth information, you may choose to perform an investigative consumer credit report, which includes a written credit report and interviews of the applicant's friends and neighbors. However, the Consumer Credit Reform Act of 1996 requires employers to obtain written permission from the applicant prior to conducting credit checks. The Act also requires employers to provide copies of the credit report to the prospective employee before taking any adverse action based on the reports.

If the applicant is denied employment because of information discovered in either type of credit report, the applicant must be provided with the name of the credit agency from which the information was obtained and must be told that the denial of the job was due to the credit report. It is illegal to deny employment because of bankruptcy.

Criminal record checks should be conducted for prospective employees who would be working with, or in close personal contact with the general public, with children, with the elderly or infirm. Criminal records should also be reviewed for candidates applying for jobs involving financial assets, including cash receipts.

According to the Equal Employment Opportunity Commission (EEOC), using criminal arrest and conviction records in making employment decisions adversely impacts Blacks and Hispanics, and therefore it is prima facie discrimination. However, you may deny employment based on a criminal conviction record if you establish a "business necessity" for the denial. You can also deny employment based on criminal arrest and conviction records if you can provide local statistics showing that such consideration does not adversely impact minorities.

If the prospective employee will be required to drive a vehicle as part of the job, check to see if there is a valid driver's license, and whether there are any driving violations. Such record checking may reduce your liability if the employee causes property damage or injury to someone while driving a company vehicle, or while driving a personal vehicle on company business.

You may also choose to check the applicant's character references, which are based on the opinions of acquaintances of the applicant. Concerns about negligent hiring are prompting employers to request more information while fear of a defamation suit is stopping some employers from responding to character references.

Consistency in your investigations is crucial to avoid unfair treatment or discrimination against a particular individual or group of individuals. A structured investigation guide will assist you to maintain consistency, even if you are using an outside investigative service. To construct the guide, you must answer the following questions.

TO DETERMINE THE APPROPRIATE INVESTIGATION, ASK YOURSELF

- Do I have the internal resources to conduct the background check myself or will I contract with an outside investigative service?
- What information on the candidate's application do I need to verify? How will I verify it?
- Do the essential functions of the job require the employee to be responsible for cash or other financial resources? If so, how will I verify the integrity of the applicant's personal financial conduct?
- Do the essential functions of the job require the employee to be in close personal contact with the general public, with children, with the elderly or infirm? How will I verify the applicant's suitability for such work?
- Do the essential functions of the job require the employee to drive a company vehicle, or drive a personal vehicle on company business? How will I verify the applicant's suitability for such work?
- Do the essential functions of the job require additional information regarding the applicant's character or activities? How will I obtain this information?

The applicant or legal representative may request a copy of the investigative report to correct errors. Therefore, documentation of the investigative process, its relationship to the job, and the results of the investigation should be kept with the application, for as long as you keep the application.

Here's how The Investigation relates to the Four Basic Principles of Effective Employee Management:

Structure: Structure is provided by the determination of the appropriate content and conduct of the investigation. Determining who will conduct the investigation, and how it will be conducted completes the framework.

Consistency: Consistency is achieved by linking all aspects of the investigation to verifying the prospective employee's ability to contribute to reaching the organization's goals.

Job-relatedness: The investigation focuses on Verifying the applicant's history as it relates to the essential functions of the job.

Documentation: The investigative process, its relationship to the job, and the results of the investigation are recorded.

Step 8: The Offer

12 Steps to Success - Step 8: The Offer

Now you are ready to communicate an offer of employment to the applicant. The offer must clearly present the conditions of employment so that the individual can make an informed decision as to whether he will accept the offer. After all, if your new employee misunderstands what the job will entail, the employee will be unhappy and leave the company. So take this opportunity to clearly communicate this important information in writing. To determine the conditions of employment, you must answer the following questions.

TO DETERMINE CONDITIONS OF EMPLOYMENT, ASK YOURSELF

- Will this employee be required to pass a pre-employment drug test?
- Will this employee be required to be examined by a company-designated health care provider?
- What will be this employee's direct compensation or "pay?"
- What will be this employee's indirect compensation or "benefits?"
- When do I expect this employee to begin work?
- What will be this employee's essential job functions?
- What will be this employee's work schedule?
- Will this employee be allowed an introductory or probationary period? What will be the length of this period? What is its purpose and what will it entail?
- Will the employee be bound by an alternative dispute resolution agreement, a non-compete agreement, a proprietary information agreement, an ethical practices commitment, or some other type of restrictive covenant? What is its purpose and what will it entail?
- Are there any company policies, such as attendance or safety policies, that should be clearly communicated at this time?
- When will the offer expire?

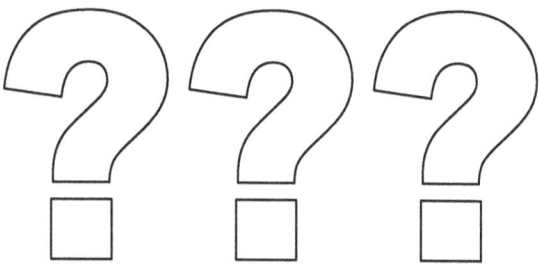

Be sure to include legally mandated conditions of employment in your offer letter. The most common of these are:
a) proper identification and authorization to work in the United States
b) work permit for individuals under 18 years old
c) completion of the Employment Eligibility Verification Form I-9
d) completion of Federal and State tax forms

In addition, the offer letter should contain a legal disclaimer to clarify the employment relationship. If your company's employment application included an explanatory statement regarding "employment-at-will," there is no need to duplicate it in the offer letter. However, if the application does not contain such a statement, the offer letter should include it. An example of such a disclaimer follows. Consult a knowledgeable employment attorney to assist you with the wording that is most appropriate for your company.

"This offer should not be construed as a guarantee of employment for any specific length of time. Employment with the company is "at-will" and can be terminated at any time and for any reason by either you or the company. This letter is not intended to be all-inclusive of company policies affecting your employment with us. Conditions of employment may be modified at any time by the company, with or without notice."

Although the candidate may accept the offer verbally, request a written acceptance as well. It can be as simple as a handwritten note and signature at the bottom of the offer letter. A written acceptance confirms that the individual accepts the conditions of employment as presented in the offer letter.

Here's how The Offer relates to the Four Basic Principles of Effective Employee Management:

Structure: The systematic process of determining the conditions of employment, and communicating them to the prospective employee in writing provides structure for the offer.

Consistency: Consistency is achieved by standardizing the offer process and linking the offer to the specific employment conditions necessary for the organization to reach its goals.

Job-relatedness: Every aspect of the offer is related to the job and working environment.

Documentation: The conditions of employment, offer and acceptance are documented.

SAMPLE OFFER LETTER

Dear Prospective Employee,

I am pleased to offer you the position of Warehouse Supervisor at an hourly rate of $xx.xx beginning March 1st. Details about our company health insurance and other benefits for which you will be eligible are enclosed.

Your employment will be contingent upon passing a drug test. In addition, all Golden Touch employees are required to be examined by a company-designated health care provider before their first day of work. You will also be expected to show proper identification and authorization to work, as well as complete the Employment Eligibility Verification Form I-9 and appropriate tax forms on your first day of work. Information about these conditions of employment are enclosed.

A copy of the Warehouse Supervisor job description and work schedule, together with information regarding our 90-day introductory period, attendance and safety policies, alternative dispute resolution program, and company code of conduct are also included in this packet.

We hope that you will accept this offer in writing by February 15th. If we have not received an answer by that date, we reserve the right to withdraw the offer. This offer is not a guarantee of employment and is not intended to be all-inclusive of company policies and conditions of employment. If you have questions about employment with us, please call me.

We look forward to hearing from you soon.

Sincerely,
Bob Golden, President

Step 9: The Hire

12 Steps to Success - Step 9: The Hire

Once the prospective employee accepts your offer, you must concentrate your efforts on ensuring that the new hire becomes a productive member of your company. Attention should be focused on providing the new hire with the information, materials, and support needed for the employee to be thoroughly integrated into your organization and become a valuable contributor to your business. A successful hire requires you to answer the following questions:

TO SUCCESSFULLY INTEGRATE THE HIRE, ASK YOURSELF

- What information does the new hire need to know about our company to successfully perform the job? How and when will this information be communicated? Who will be involved in communicating this information?
- What job-related training will the new hire need to successfully perform his job? How will this training be conducted? Who will conduct the training? When will the training be conducted?
- What supplies, equipment, or other materials does the new hire need to successfully perform the job? How will the employee obtain these materials? When will the employee obtain these materials?
- Will the new hire need instruction in the proper use of supplies, equipment, or other materials to successfully perform the job? Who will provide the instruction? When will the instruction be conducted?

How will I make this new hire feel welcome? Who should be involved in this welcoming process? When will it be conducted?

The answers to these questions form what is typically referred to as "New Employee Orientation." The orientation should begin on the first day of employment, but the length of orientation will vary according to your needs and the needs of the new hire. Some of the most common elements of a new employee orientation include:

a) Completion of legally required paperwork such as the Employment Eligibility Verification Form I-9, Employee's Withholding Allowance Certificate Form W-4, and appropriate state tax forms
b) Description of the job and its role in the organization
c) Explanation of company policies and procedures
d) Explanation of pay, including administrative items such as when paychecks are issued
e) Explanation of, and enrollment in employee benefit plans
f) Tour of the facility and area to which the new employee is assigned
g) Issuing uniform, locker, time card, personal safety equipment and other supplies, equipment, and materials.
h) Completion of legally required safety training, such as Hazardous Materials Communication (also known as Right-to-Know training) and Bloodborne Pathogens training.
i) Matching the new hire with an experienced co-worker or "mentor" to facilitate integration into the organization.

A written orientation program provides the basis for a consistent process, resulting in an efficient integration of new employees into your organization. In addition, a written orientation program enables you to easily evaluate its effectiveness, and revise it as needed.

Documentation of the entire orientation process is also an excellent historical record. It can be used in assessing performance expectations and development needs, as well as

confirmation that critical and legally required information has been communicated. Orientation documents should include:
a) the information communicated during the orientation, the method by which it was communicated, and the individual(s) responsible for the communication
b) the dates and times of the orientation
c) a list of supplies, equipment, and materials assigned to the new employee
d) a record of orientation activities, such as a tour, or lunch with co-workers
e) the name of the new hire's mentor
f) a record that the following documents have been signed: Employee's Withholding Allowance Certificate Form W-4 and appropriate state tax forms, Employment Eligibility Verification Form I-9, benefit enrollment forms (where applicable), payroll deduction authorization (where applicable), restrictive covenants (where applicable), receipt for company property (where applicable), receipt for employee handbook (where applicable), certification that applicable training and/or instruction was conducted, certification that company policies, procedures, rules, and regulations were explained, and other applicable documents signed by the new employee

> ### *Here's how The Hire relates to the Four Basic Principles of Effective Employee Management:*
>
> **Structure**: The foundation of the structure consists of the systematic determination of the information, materials, and support needed to facilitate the new hire's integration into the organization. Determining how and when the information, materials, and support will be provided, and by whom it will be provided completes the framework.
>
> **Consistency**: The orientation provides a similar orientation experience to all new hires and concentrates on ensuring the new hire effectively contributes to the organization's goals.
>
> **Job-relatedness**: The information, materials, and support provided to the new hire during this process are directly related to the ability to perform the job.
>
> **Documentation**: The orientation program and process are written, including who, what, where, and when the information was communicated. Records of all signed documents, including state and federal tax and employment eligibility forms, and company-related forms are retained.

Step 10: The Appraisal

12 Steps to Success - Step 10: The Appraisal

Every day the employee works with you provides an opportunity to evaluate his or her contribution to the organization's goals. Continual performance appraisal is the most effective way to encourage desired behavior, and quickly identify and improve non-productive behavior. To accomplish this, you must first answer these questions.

TO EFFECTIVELY EVALUATE PERFORMANCE, ASK YOURSELF

- Is the employee consistently performing the essential functions of the job?
- If the employee is consistently performing the essential functions of the job, exactly what knowledge, skills, abilities, traits, and behaviors does the employee possess that enables him or her to do this?
- Aside from those behaviors necessary to successfully perform his job, does the employee exhibit cooperative, creative, leadership, or other behaviors you would like to encourage?
- If the employee is not consistently performing the essential functions of the job, which functions is he or she failing to perform?
- What knowledge, skills, abilities, traits, and behaviors does the employee lack, thus preventing successful performance?
- Is the employee exhibiting non-productive, undesirable, and or destructive behavior unrelated to the performance of the essential functions of the job that you would like to discourage?

A written history of performance is the foundation for increasing the employee's contribution to organizational goals. Beginning with the first day of work, critical incidents should be noted. Remember to notice good performance as well as areas for improvement.

To encourage desired behavior and assist the employee to correct deficiencies in performance, you must answer the following questions.

TO INCREASE CONTRIBUTION TO ORGANIZATIONAL GOALS, ASK YOURSELF

- If the employee is consistently performing the essential functions of the job, how will I encourage the employee to continue doing so?
- What cooperative, creative, leadership, or other behaviors would I like to encourage and how will I encourage the employee to develop them?
- If the employee is not consistently performing the essential functions of the job, how can I assist the employee to develop the knowledge, skills, abilities, traits, and behaviors necessary to improve performance?
- How will I discourage any non-productive, undesirable, or destructive behaviors being exhibited by the employee?

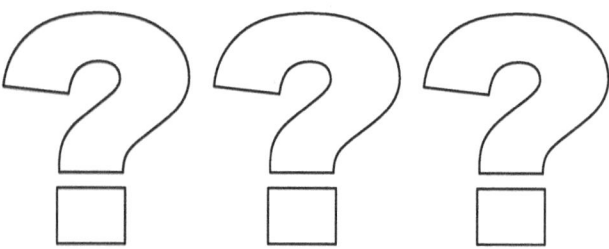

The answers to these questions become part of the collaborative effort of you and the employee to improve performance. Collaboration requires communication and effective communication is the key to a successful performance appraisal and improvement process. Effective performance communication includes:
1. Clearly defined expectations of performance and behavior
2. Specific examples of successful performance, or failure to perform and resulting consequences
3. Specific examples of behaviors you would like to encourage or discourage, and resulting consequences
4. Continual feedback that allows for immediate recognition of desired performance and behavior, and quick identification of areas where improvement is needed
5. Formal performance discussions with the employee at regular intervals, including a written performance appraisal and improvement document

An effective performance appraisal and improvement document consists of the history of performance and behavior, how that performance and behavior relates to the job and your expectations, and the collaborative effort to improve performance and behavior. It serves as a record of your discussion with the employee, as well as a written commitment between both parties to agreed-upon actions that will result in a greater contribution to the organization's goals.

Your signature on the document, as well as that of the employee, signifies a joint commitment to reaching the organization's goals. Obtain the employee's signature on all written performance reviews. If nothing else, it verifies that the employee has seen the written performance evaluation. If the employee is hesitant, or refuses to sign, request a neutral third party to witness that the employee has been informed of his or her performance and include documentation to that effect.

Here's how The Appraisal relates to the Four Basic Principles of Effective Employee Management:

Structure: The structure consists of the history of performance and behavior, how that performance and behavior relates to the job and your expectations, and the plan to improve performance and behavior.

Consistency: Consistency is achieved by linking all aspects of performance and behavior to their contribution to organizational goals.

Job-relatedness: Job-related performance and behavior is observed, recorded, and communicated to the employee. Improvement efforts are focused on job-related performance and behavior.

Documentation: The history of performance and behavior, how that performance and behavior relates to the job and your expectations, the plan to improve performance and behavior, and the communication of this information is captured in writing.

Step 11: The Discipline

12 Steps to Success - Step 11: The Discipline

The performance appraisal process usually brings three scenarios to the forefront.
1. The employee is doing what he or she should be doing, which we'll call "good performance."
2. The employee is not doing what he or she should be doing, which we'll call "poor performance."
3. The employee is doing something he or she should not be doing, which we'll call "misconduct."

Poor performance and misconduct do not contribute to the organization's goals. You must assist employees to modify their performance and behavior or terminate their employment.

Corrective action, or discipline is one form of behavior modification. In the case of poor performance, discipline may be appropriate when the collaborative efforts of you and the employee to improve performance through education and skill development have not resulted in the desired outcome. Discipline may also be appropriate in cases of misconduct where the employee is demonstrating unproductive, undesirable, or destructive behavior in violation of company policy or the law. To determine if discipline is appropriate, you must answer these questions.

TO DETERMINE WHEN DISCIPLINE IS APPROPRIATE, ASK YOURSELF

Poor performance:

- Did you clearly communicate your performance expectations to the employee? How were those expectations communicated? When were they communicated?
- Are these performance standards applied uniformly for all employees?
- Did you clearly communicate the consequences of not meeting your performance expectations to the employee? How and when were these consequences communicated?
- Are these consequences applied uniformly for all employees?
- What specific actions have been taken to improve performance through education and skill development? Are there additional opportunities to improve performance through education and skill development?

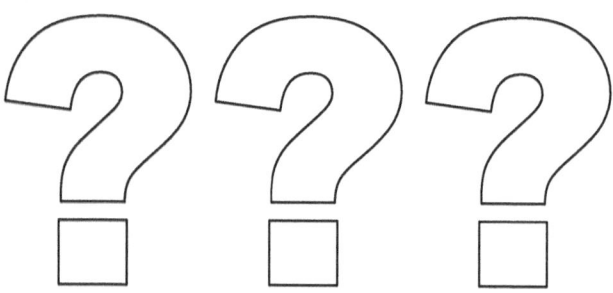

TO DETERMINE WHEN DISCIPLINE IS APPROPRIATE, ASK YOURSELF

Misconduct:

- Did you clearly communicate your behavior expectations to the employee? How were those expectations communicated? When were they communicated?
- Are these behavior standards applied uniformly for all employees?
- Did you clearly communicate the consequences of not meeting your behavior expectations to the employee? How were those consequences communicated? When were they communicated?
- Are these consequences applied uniformly for all employees?
- What specific actions have you taken to investigate the facts surrounding the employee's behavior? What facts did that investigation disclose?

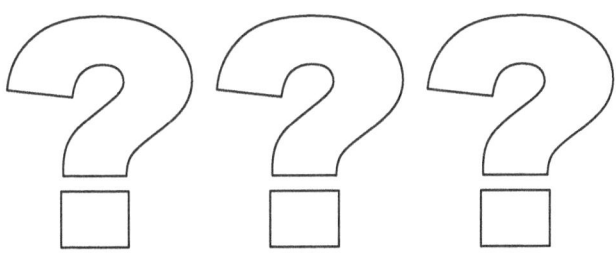

The corrective action you take is a reflection of your company's internal culture. Your disciplinary process may be long or short, positive or punitive. However you design the specifics, the process should include:
a) an initial communication to the employee expressing that his or her performance or behavior is unacceptable. This communication should also include the consequences of continued poor performance or misconduct and the time frame in which you expect improvement. Improvement should be specific and measurable.
b) a second communication to the employee expressing that his or her performance or behavior is still unacceptable. This communication should stress the consequences of continued poor performance or misconduct and the time frame in which you expect improvement. Improvement should be specific and measurable.
c) a specific period of time for the employee to focus on performance or behavior, his or her role in the organization, and whether the employee wishes to remain employed with the company.
d) termination of employment.

There are as many variations on discipline as there are employers. However, there are some basic points in common:
1. Discipline should be consistently applied to all employees.
2. Discipline should be discussed in a private meeting with the employee, the employee's immediate supervisor, and a neutral mediator when appropriate.
3. Every disciplinary discussion should be documented. It should clearly state the undesired behavior and the desired behavior, as well as the consequences of the employee's actions. Furthermore, it should include both your views and the employee's views expressed during the discussion.

4. Every disciplinary document should be signed by both you and the employee, and the neutral mediator when appropriate. The signatures act as an acknowledgment of receipt and a commitment to modifying the behavior. If the employee is hesitant, or refuses to sign, request a neutral third party to witness that the discussion took place and include documentation to that effect.
5. Records of disciplinary actions should not remain in the file of an active employee indefinitely. Most employees either improve their performance or behavior within 12 months or they are fired. Therefore, if the employee improves performance or behavior sufficiently to meet your expectations and successfully perform the essential functions of the job, it makes sense to discard such documents after 12 months.
6. Disciplinary actions, including terminations resulting from an employee's performance or behavior should not be communicated by management to other employees as some sort of deterrant to similar performance or behavior problems. Discipline is a private and confidential matter between management and the affected employee.

Once you design the disciplinary process that is appropriate for your organization, you must capture it in writing. Documentation of the process helps to ensure that it is communicated and administered consistently to all employees. It is also easier to review and change the process if it is documented.

> ***Here's how The Discipline relates to the Four Basic Principles of Effective Employee Management***
>
> **Structure**: Structure is provided in the determination of the appropriateness of discipline, and the design of the process.
>
> **Consistency**: Discipline is applied consistently to all employees and concentrates on performance and behaviors affecting the company's goals.
>
> **Job-relatedness**: Discipline focuses on the performance of the essential functions of the job and the expected behaviors while performing that job.
>
> **Documentation**: The discipline process and every disciplinary discussion is documented.

SAMPLE POLICY - STANDARDS OF CONDUCT

I. PURPOSE

To assure safe, efficient and harmonious operations and to fully inform all employees of their responsibilities in this regard.

II. SCOPE

This policy applies to employees at all locations.

III. POLICY

Golden Touch Enterprises' standards of conduct are established for the guidance of all employees. The following represents only a partial list of unacceptable behaviors and conduct, as a complete list of all possible violations would be impossible to write.

Infractions will lead to corrective action up to and including discharge.

IV. BREACHES OF STANDARDS OF CONDUCT (Partial List)

1. Use, possession, sale, purchase, transfer or being under the influence of alcoholic beverages, illegal drugs or other intoxicants at any time on company premises or while on company business.
2. Falsifying employment application, timecard, personnel, or other company documents or records.
3. Unauthorized possession of company or other employee property, gambling, carrying weapons or explosives, or violating criminal laws on company premises.
4. Fighting, throwing things, horseplay, practical jokes or other disorderly conduct.
5. Engaging in acts of dishonesty, fraud, theft or sabotage.
6. Threatening, intimidating, coercing, using abusive or vulgar language, or interfering with the performance of other employees.
7. Insubordination or refusal to comply with instructions or failure to perform reasonable duties which are assigned.

1. Unauthorized use of company material, time, equipment or property.
2. Damaging or destroying company property through careless or willful acts.
3. Conduct which the company feels reflects adversely on the employee or company.
4. Performance which, in the company's opinion, does not meet the requirements of the position.
5. Engaging in such other practices as the company determines may be inconsistent with the ordinary and reasonable rules of conduct necessary to the welfare of the company, its employees or clients.
6. Negligence in observing fire prevention and safety rules.
7. Other circumstances for which the company feels that corrective action is warranted.

SAMPLE POLICY - DISCIPLINARY/CORRECTIVE ACTION

I. PURPOSE

To set forth general supervisory guidelines for a corrective action process aimed to document and correct undesirable employee behavior.

II. SCOPE

This policy applies to departments, supervisors and employees in all locations.

III. POLICY

Golden Touch Enterprises seeks to establish and maintain standards of employee conduct and supervisory practices which will, in the interest of the company and its employees, support and promote effective business operations. Such supervisory practices include administering corrective action when employee conduct or performance problems arise.

Major elements of this policy generally include:

A. Constructive effort by the supervisor to help employees achieve fully satisfactory standards of conduct and job performance.

B. Correcting employee shortcomings or negative behavior to the extent required.

C. Notice to employees through communicating this policy that discharge will result from continued or gross violation of employee standards of conduct or unsatisfactory job performance.

D. Written documentation of disciplinary warnings given and corrective measures taken.

E. Documentation of corrective action will become part of the employee's personnel record for a period of 12 months. If no related disciplinary measures are recorded within that period, the documentation will be removed from the file.

IV. OPTIONS FOR CORRECTIVE ACTION

Depending on the facts and circumstances involved in each situation, management may choose to begin corrective action at any step up to and including immediate discharge. However, in most cases, the following steps should be followed:

A. Verbal Warning. For infractions the company deems to be minor, the employee should at a minimum be issued a verbal warning.

B. Written Warning. For repeated minor infractions, or a more substantial infraction, the employee should at a minimum be issued a written warning. If the situation does not improve within a reasonable time (not longer than four months, depending on the seriousness of the issue), the supervisor may repeat the measure or take steps to discharge the employee.

The written warning should be prepared following a corrective action discussion with the employee. The employee will be given an opportunity to comment in writing and should be asked to sign a copy of the warning, acknowledging receipt. Three copies of the warning will be distributed as follows:

(1) employee;
(2) supervisor;
(3) personnel file.

C. Discharge. For infractions management deems to be sufficiently serious, or continued failure to respond appropriately to prior corrective action, discharge is appropriate.

V. OTHER OPTION FOR CORRECTIVE ACTION

Suspension. If events compel a supervisor to take immediate action when discharge appears possible, the supervisor will immediately suspend the employee for a specified period, pending an investigation. The employee will be required to leave the premises immediately. The manager will be notified immediately. The suspension / investigation period will last no longer than three working days, except in highly unusual circumstances. The objective of this suspension will be to determine if discharge is the proper decision.

SAMPLE POLICY - COMPLAINT PROCEDURE

I. PURPOSE
To provide a process for employees to discuss complaints or problems with management and to receive careful consideration and a prompt resolution.

II. SCOPE
This policy applies to non-union employees at domestic locations.

III. POLICY
Each employee of the company is encouraged to:
a) Discuss work-related complaints or problems with management
b) Appeal an unfavorable decision to a higher authority in the company
c)

IV. DEFINITION
"Complaint" is defined as a condition of employment or application of a policy that the employee thinks is unjust or inequitable.

V. PROCEDURE
A. Supervisor's Role. To resolve complaints and problems, the employee is encouraged to first seek assistance from his or her immediate supervisor, who should attempt to resolve the problem. The supervisor is responsible to handle the complaint as an important business matter, striving to arrive at a prompt, equitable solution.

B. Alternative Channels. Occasionally, an employee's complaint involves his or her supervisor. Supervisors should realize that employees often do not feel free to express such concerns to them. Therefore, employees are encouraged to discuss complaints with the next higher level of management to avoid an awkward situation. As an alternative, the employee may discuss the complaint at any time with the human resources manager. An employee may ask the human resources manager, another employee or another manager to be present at a complaint discussion with any level of management.

C. Appeals. If the employee's complaint is not settled satisfactorily with the immediate supervisor, the employee is encouraged to appeal the complaint to the next higher level of management. The company expects supervisors to support this appeal process to help rectify any remaining dissatisfaction.

The employee may appeal a complaint through succeeding levels of management to the General Manager, if desired. The General Manager will render a final decision on the matter after appropriate investigations.

Step 12: The Termination

12 Steps to Success - Step 12: The Termination

Termination of employment falls into two categories:
1. Voluntary termination which includes resignation and retirement
2. Involuntary termination which includes firing, permanent lay-off, and death

Both types of terminations share some common concerns for employers, such as insurance, the morale of remaining employees, and legal requirements. Although most employers concentrate their concern on the "right" way to fire an employee, it is equally as important to properly handle the other types of terminations. Appropriate action during the termination process requires that you answer the following questions.

TO DETERMINE YOUR TERMINATION ACTION PLAN, ASK YOURSELF

Voluntary resignations:

- Why is the employee leaving the company? How was that information communicated to you? When did you receive this information?
- When will the employee leave the company? Are there security reasons that require the employee to leave immediately, or can the employee continue to work until the intended departure date?
- Will the employee retain all security privileges until the last day of work?
- Are there projects yet to be finished by the employee? Who will assume responsibility for completion?
- Will there be a transition process to another employee? Do you expect the employee to train this replacement?
- Does the employee want you to notify co-workers, or would the employee rather communicate it? Is a farewell luncheon or other event appropriate?
- When will an exit interview to discuss working conditions, interpersonal relationships with supervisors, co-workers, and subordinates, and suggestions for improvement be conducted? Who will conduct the exit interview?

If termination is due to poor performance:
- Were the essential functions of the job clearly communicated to the employee?
- Were your performance expectations clearly communicated to the employee?
- Were the consequences of continued poor performance clearly communicated to the employee?
- What collaborative efforts were made to improve knowledge and skills to enable the employee to successfully perform the job?
- Was the disciplinary process conducted in a thorough, consistent manner?
- Are all performance-related communications and activities documented, signed and dated by you and the employee?

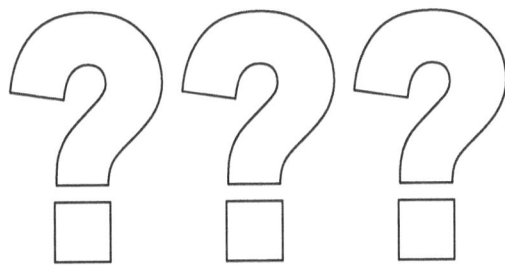

If termination is due to misconduct:
- Were your expectations of acceptable and unacceptable conduct clearly communicated to the employee?
- Were the consequences of misconduct clearly communicated to the employee?
- Was the misconduct thoroughly, fairly, objectively investigated?
- Did you obtain the employee's account of what happened?
- Was the disciplinary process conducted in a thorough, consistent manner?
- Are all conduct-related communications and activities documented, signed and dated by you and the employee?

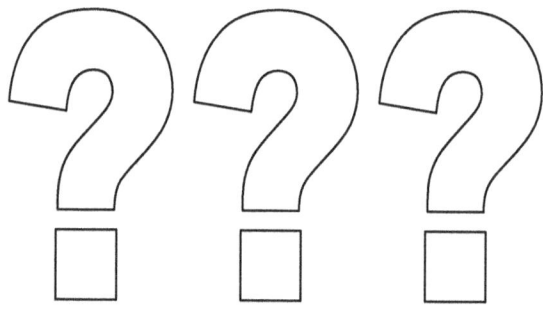

For all terminations, regardless of reason:
- Does the company owe the employee any compensation, such as unused vacation?
- Does the employee have company property in his possession or owe the company any money? How and when will the employee return this property or repay the loan? Has the employee signed an authorization to deduct the value of unreturned property or unpaid loans when he or she leaves?
- If your company is subject to COBRA, when and how will you inform the employee of his COBRA rights? When and how will you inform the employee's dependents of their rights?
- Does the employee have life insurance or other insurance through the company? What is the status of that policy and what are the employee's options to continue the policy? How and when will you communicate this information to the employee? In the case of employee death, how and when will you communicate this information to the employee's beneficiaries?
- Does the employee have vested retirement savings? What is the status of that retirement account and what are the employee's options? How and when will you communicate this information to the employee and, if appropriate, the employee's spouse? In the case of employee death, how and when will you communicate this information to the employee's beneficiaries?

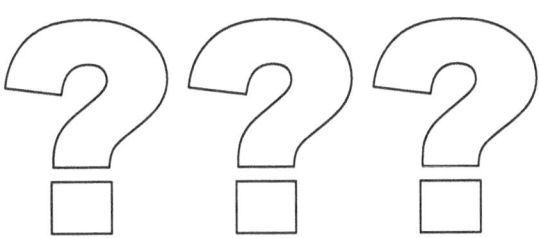

The reason for termination of employment should always be documented. For example, if it is a resignation, require a letter from the employee stating the reason for departure.

If you fire an employee, you must document the entire process leading to the termination, including steps taken to avoid firing the individual. The termination documents should be presented to the employee in a private meeting with the immediate supervisor and a neutral mediator. The content of the documents should be explained thoroughly. Once again, documents should be signed by all parties.

Exit interviews are useful, and should be done whenever an employee leaves your company, voluntarily or not. But like employment interviews, it is best to structure the discussion with an exit interview guide. Here are some suggestions:

Exit Interview DOs:

1. The exit interview should be conducted with two neutral parties gathering information from the departing employee. The employee's supervisor should not be involved in the exit interview.
2. If you are offering the employee a severance package that contains releases of liability, be sure to explain the details of the package.
3. Notify the employee of his or her rights under COBRA (if applicable).
4. Provide information about unemployment compensation. You can usually get free brochures from your state's employment office.
5. Listen carefully and patiently to what the employee has to say, and remain neutral regarding complaints.
6. Arrange for the return of company documents or property.
7. Remind the employee that he or she has a continuing obligation to maintain the confidentiality of the company's business even after leaving the company.

8. Make arrangements for the employee to remove personal belongings at your mutual convenience.
9. Confirm that the employee's compensation records are accurate. Pay the employee for all accrued compensation, including salary, vacation time and commissions.

Exit Interview DON'Ts:

1. Do not argue with the employee.
2. Do not say or suggest that the departing employee is incompetent or dishonest. Such statements increase your legal liability for defamation.
3. Other than ineligibility to receive the offered severance package, do not suggest any sort of negative consequence resulting from failure to sign the severance agreement.
4. Do not promise the employee a good recommendation or help in getting another job. If someone asks for a good recommendation, consult with a knowledgeable attorney about your course of action.
5. Do not try to spare the departing employee's feelings by giving a false reason for the termination.
6. Do not respond to accusations of improper or illegal behavior without counsel from a knowledgeable attorney.

Your termination duties do not end once the employee leaves the company. There may be administrative activities relating to such things as employment verifications or reference checks, unemployment compensation, insurance, and retirement benefits. Or there may be the ordeal of defending the company against a breach of contract, wrongful discharge, or discrimination lawsuit.

Dealing with requests for employment verifications and references is the most common post-termination activity. You have probably had it drilled into you that the only information you should give during a reference check is name, dates of employment, and job title. Heaven forbid you should give a negative reference lest you be taken to court for defamation.

Add to that the U. S. Supreme Court decision in *Robinson v. Shell Oil Inc.* that employers can be held liable for retaliation if they give negative references for former employees who have sought protection under Title VII of the Civil Rights Act of 1964, and negative references get really risky.

In the case referenced above, Charles Robinson, a black sales representative was fired by Shell Oil Company. After his termination, Robinson filed a discrimination complaint with the Equal Employment Opportunity Commission (EEOC). When he was rejected for a job with another company, Robinson sued Shell Oil, claiming that a company sales manager had given a negative job reference to his prospective employer in retaliation for the EEOC complaint. The court ruled in Robinson's favor.

As a result, employers must protect themselves not only from defamation charges, but also from discrimination, retaliation, and other civil rights violations when disclosing information about former employees.

Is it a better idea to ignore the negative and accentuate the positive when giving references? Not necessarily. In *Randi W. v. Muroc Joint Unified School District,* the California Supreme Court ruled that employers that write letters of recommendation for former employees may not omit negative information regarding qualifications and character if there is a foreseeable risk of physical injury to the prospective employer or third parties.

In this particular case, officials at three public schools where the applicant worked each gave favorable written references. None of them mentioned that their former employee had been the subject of parent complaints and student accusations of sexual harassment and misconduct. He was hired as a vice principal where, according to the suit, he molested a 13-year-old student. The court ruled against the school district, implying that even though there was no proof behind the complaints and accusations, the information should have been released.

If it is risky to give information, and it is risky not to give information, what is an employer supposed to do? There is no law or court ruling that requires an employer to provide references. However, if you choose to provide references for former employees, there are ways to reduce, but not eliminate your liability.

1. Institute a "post-termination inquiry" policy that designates specific individuals authorized to respond to such inquiries and precisely what information they are authorized to release. All requests for employment verification and references should be directed to these authorized individuals.
2. Require that all reference requests must be in writing and accompanied by a signed legal release to provide the requested information. You can go one step further and provide your own authorization form releasing your company from any liability and require that the former employee sign it.
3. Retain a copy of the written reference request, the authorization to release the information, and your written response.
4. Keep references neutral. Provide factual, documented data. If the former employee displayed behavior that could result in a foreseeable risk of physical injury to the prospective employer or third parties, consult with a knowledgeable employment attorney regarding your course of action.
5. Qualify references with appropriate legal disclaimers. An example of a disclaimer follows. Consult a knowledgeable employment attorney to assist you with the wording that is most appropriate for your company.

"The enclosed reference information is limited to documented file data and is strictly confidential. It is not, nor is it intended to be all inclusive. The Company will not be held liable for omissions, unintentional or otherwise. Information contained in this report is not to be construed as an endorsement or recommendation for employment."

Another common post-termination activity is responding to claims for unemployment compensation. Undeserved unemployment compensation payments can be costly. Therefore, it is important to understand how unemployment compensation is administered and how you can minimize being charged for undeserved payments.

The Federal Unemployment Tax Act was introduced in 1935. The program that resulted from the Act is financed through the contributions of employers, which are actually taxes based on the employer's annual payroll and past history of unemployment among its workers. This sliding tax schedule is called a "merit rating" or an "experience rating." An employer's experience rating is based on a ratio of experience with unemployment and total payroll. Thus, the cost to the employer is directly influenced by the number of successful claims against the employer in the past.

Although initiated by the Federal government, unemployment insurance is regulated on the state level. Typically, the state requires the unemployed individual to file a claim with the state employment commission to receive benefits. After the commission notifies the employer of the claim, the employer must respond with a "noncharging request" within the prescribed time limit. The noncharging request must provide sufficient factual information to show clearly and conclusively that the claimant either quit voluntarily without good cause attributable to the employer, or was discharged for misconduct connected with the work, or discharged for substantial fault connected with the work. Factual information may include your company policy, disciplinary actions, resignation letters, exit interview form or other appropriate documentation.

Each claim is determined individually. If the noncharging request is timely and acceptable in all respects, the commission may rule that the employer's experience rating account will not be charged for any benefits. However, if the noncharging request is not timely, or sufficient factual evidence regarding termination of employment is not presented, the claim will be charged against the employer's experience rating.

But what about that termination monster every employer fears - the lawsuit? It is true that the number of employment-related litigation cases has skyrocketed in recent years. No employer is immune to this epidemic. However, it is important to remember that most employment law is based on the Four Basic Principles of Effective Employee Management. The strength of your company's defense will be greatly enhanced if your employment and termination processes are based on those same principles.

Here's how The Termination relates to the Four Basic Principles of Effective Employee Management:

Structure: The systematic process of determining an appropriate termination action plan provides structure to the termination.

Consistency: Consistency is achieved by ensuring the termination process is administered similarly for similar situations and relating all aspects of the process to organizational goals.

Job-relatedness: The termination process focuses on the employee's failure to display the knowledge, skills, abilities, and behaviors required to successfully perform the essential functions of the job.

Documentation: The termination action plan, exit interview, disciplinary actions, reasons for termination, and related discussions are documented.

CHAPTER IV

The Result
Conclusion

Whoa! This program is not easy!

Conclusion

It is true that the 12-Step Employment Program for Small Businesses is challenging. It is also true that The Program works. If you follow The Program within the confines of The Rules and within the framework of the Four Basic Principles of Effective Employee Management, you will have an efficient, cost-effective, and legal employment process that will allow you to recruit, select, and retain employees that will make a positive contribution to the success of your business.

The result is up to you. It is your solution to your dilemma. It is of your design to meet your unique situation, and can be changed as your needs change.

You *can* hire and keep good employees, and you *can* get rid of the not-so-good ones. Now get out there and do it!

The Appendix

The Internet - Web sites containing workplace information

The Posters - Federally mandated posters for the workplace

The Records - Federally required recordkeeping guidelines

The Appendix

The Internet

The following Internet sites may assist you in learning more about the employment process. (Note: Due to the nature of the Internet, web sites change frequently.)

The Society for Human Resource Management (SHRM) site includes comprehensive human resource data and numerous links to other employment-related sites - www.shrm.org

The Institute of Management and Administration (IOMA) site includes human resource data and links to other employment-related sites - www.ioma.com

The Bureau of Labor Statistics offers information on employment trends - http://stats.bls.gov

The Employment Statistics Home Page provided by the Community College of Allegheny County is an online worksheet that allows you to perform disparate impact calculations and other employment-related statistical analyses quickly and easily - www.acd.ccac.edu/hr/EmploymentStatistics/

Curry Business System's Employment Interviewer Training Course is a comprehensive and free guide to effective interviewing - www.curryinc.com

Training.Net is dedicated to training and development issues, including special reports and interactive bulletin boards - www.trainingnet.com

The Center for Mobility Resource's Salary Calculator allows you to calculate the salary needed in the new location to maintain the employee's current standard of living - www.homefair.com/homefair/cmr/salcalc.html)

The Research Institute of America site offers compensation, benefits, safety, news, analyses, and forecasts - www.insidehr.com

Law Journal Extra's Employment and Labor Law Update features employment law and court decisions - www.ljextra.com/practice/laboremployment/labcol.html

LawCrawler searches the Internet for court findings and articles on legal topics - www.lawcrawler.com

The United States Department of Labor site offers access to all federal employment laws and regulations, statistics, and data - www.dol.gov

The HRnet Web Center is a forum for discussing workplace issues and sharing best practices - www.the-hrnet.com

The Posters

Federal employment regulations require the following posters to be displayed prominently in the workplace. All federal posters, with the exception of the Equal Employment Opportunity Commission poster, can be obtained by contacting the U. S. Department of Labor. The EEO poster may be obtained by contacting the Equal Employment Opportunity Commission Publications Information Center at 800 669-EEOC. All of the following posters are free.

ALL EMPLOYERS:
- "Polygraph Protection Act Notice"
- Minimum wage and hours of work poster known as "Your Rights"

EMPLOYERS WITH 15 OR MORE EMPLOYEES:
- "Equal Employment Opportunity is the Law"

EMPLOYERS WITH 50 OR MORE EMPLOYEES:
- "Your Rights Under The Family And Medical Leave Act of 1993"

EMPLOYERS WITH FEDERAL CONSTRUCTION CONTRACTS IN EXCESS OF $2500:
- "Notice to Employees Working on Federal or Federally Financed Construction Projects"

EMPLOYERS WITH FEDERAL CONTRACTS IN EXCESS OF $10,000:
- "Notice to Employees Working on Government Contracts"

The Records

The following recordkeeping guidelines apply to Federal requirements and are not intended to be all-inclusive. State requirements may require you to keep records for a longer period of time than indicated below. Please consult with the appropriate Federal and State officials or a knowledgeable employment attorney regarding the appropriate recordkeeping requirements for your company.

a) Employee pay records and related documentation should be kept for three (3) years.
b) Employment Eligibility Verification Form I-9 should be kept for three (3) years after hire or one (1) year after termination, whichever is later.
c) Occupational Safety and Health Act (OSHA) logs, summaries, records of individual injuries and illnesses and related records should be kept for five (5) years.
d) Documentation of hires, promotions, terminations and other personnel actions should be kept for one (1) year after the action.
e) EEO - 1 forms should be kept for one (1) year.
f) Records pertinent to a discrimination claim under Title VII of the Civil Rights Act of 1964, the Americans with Disabilities Act (ADA), or other employment laws should be kept until the claim is concluded.
g) Benefit plans and seniority and merit system information should be kept for the life of the plan plus one (1) year.
h) Records pertaining to leaves under the Family and Medical Leave Act must be kept for three (3) years.
i) Under the Employee Retirement Income Security Act (ERISA), retirement plan descriptions and related documents should be kept for six (6) years after the documents were produced.
j) Records regarding eligibility of retirement plan participants should be kept for the life of the plan and until pending legal action is concluded.

About the Author

Patricia G. Pollack has assisted companies with workplace issues since 1977. Her down-to-earth views and practical advice to small business owners have appeared in newspapers, business journals, and magazines nationwide. Formerly the host of a daily radio show on workplace issues, Ms. Pollack is often called upon to share her ideas regarding human resource management on radio and television news programs. Her dynamic and informative presentation style has made her a popular and highly sought-after speaker on the employer-employee relationship and its variables.

Ms. Pollack is a Phi Beta Kappa graduate of the University of Tennessee, where she received her Bachelor's Degree in Business Administration, specializing in Personnel Management. She continued her education at Georgia State University, where she received her Masters of Business Administration, specializing in Industrial Relations.

Founder and former president of The HRNetwork, LLC, a human resources consulting, education, and publishing firm, Ms. Pollack currently acts as executive director of the Metrolina Entrepreneurial Council, Inc. in Charlotte, North Carolina. The Metrolina Entrepreneurial Council is a non-profit business association for owners of high growth businesses.

www.ingramcontent.com/pod-product-compliance
Lightning Source LLC
Chambersburg PA
CBHW021543200526
45163CB00014B/845